# You Don't Have to Dread Cafeteria Duty

Dedicated to every classroom teacher or staff member who has ever dreaded cafeteria, bus, or recess duty; to every compassionate administrator who has ever tried to help; and to every child who has ever felt fear or distress at the idea of eating lunch in the school cafeteria or playing on the playground.

# You Don't Have to Dread Cafeteria Duty

## A Guide to Surviving Lunchroom, Recess, Bus, and "Other Duties as Assigned"

**Dori E. Novak**
**Joanne C. Strohmer**

**CORWIN PRESS, INC.**
A Sage Publications Company
Thousand Oaks, California

*For information:*

Corwin Press, Inc.
A Sage Publications Company
2455 Teller Road
Thousand Oaks, California 91320
E-mail: order@corwinpress.com

SAGE Publications Ltd.
6 Bonhill Street
London EC2A 4PU
United Kingdom

SAGE Publications India Pvt. Ltd.
M-32 Market
Greater Kailash I
New Delhi 110 048 India

Printed in the United States of America

**Library of Congress Cataloging-in-Publication Data**

Novak, Dori E.
    You don't have to dread cafeteria duty : A guide to surviving lunchroom, recess, bus, and "other duties as assigned" / Dori E. Novak, Joanne C. Strohmer.
        p.     cm.
    ISBN 0-8039-6734-9 (cloth : acid-free paper)
    ISBN 0-8039-6735-7 (pbk. : acid-free paper)
    1. Teachers—Workload—United States.   2. School lunchrooms, cafeterias, etc.—United States.   3. Recesses—United States. 4. School environment—United States.   I. Strohmer, Joanne C. II. Title.
    LB2844.1.W6 N68   1998
    371.14'14—ddc21                                    98-9027

This book is printed on acid-free paper.

98  99  00  01  02  03  10  9  8  7  6  5  4  3  2  1

Production Editor: S. Marlene Head
Editorial Assistant: Kristen L. Gibson
Typesetter: Andrea D. Swanson
Cover Designer: Marcia M. Rosenburg

# Contents

# Preface

Dear Duty Dreaders,

Think of all the times you have headed down the hallway toward the school cafeteria to report for lunch duty. Remember the dread you felt. Recall the knot in your stomach. Recollect the sigh of relief that escaped your lips when the last child filed out of the room.

We are here to tell you that it does not have to be that way. School lunch periods can be relaxing midday breaks. They can be comfortable and fun for both young diners and their adult hosts. And we are not saying these things because we have been sipping the cooking sherry. The ideas in this book have been tested in public schools and have been proven to work.

*You Don't Have to Dread Cafeteria Duty* is designed to inspire you to think in a new way. The book will help you transform your school's cafeteria into a pleasant school restaurant without spending a lot of money. Each chapter will give you lots of concrete ideas to prime your thinking about how to enhance the ambiance of your lunchroom and how to improve the behavior of young diners. As you read along, you will see how transforming your cafeteria will not only make lunchtime more enjoyable but also give children a chance to learn and practice social and thinking skills. As a bonus, we have included a chapter about surviving other duties you may dread.

## Who Will Enjoy Reading This Book

This book was written for elementary school administrators, cafeteria staff, custodians, assistants, guidance counselors, and teachers who deal with youngsters in cafeteria, hallway, and playground settings. Middle school educators will also find they can adapt ideas in this book to their situations.

In addition, parent-teacher organizations and other parent volunteers can use this book. Parents want their children to have enjoyable school meals and play periods so they are refreshed for their afternoon classes. A little group of parents might study the ideas in *You Don't Have to Dread Cafeteria Duty* and inspire others in the school to get started on a cafeteria transformation project.

## What You Will Find in This Book

This book is packed with ideas about the kinds of changes you can make to transform cafeteria and other duties. There is lots of information about how to bring about the changes and have fun at the same time. Chapter 1 will help you begin the process of looking at the current situation in detail. You will have a chance to see if there are some aspects that you want to preserve because they are working well. Even more importantly, you will have an opportunity to examine the specific elements that distress you.

In Chapter 2, the fun starts. You will be invited to create a vision of what could be. After you have a concrete picture in mind, Chapter 3 will assist you in considering who could help make your dream for the cafeteria come true. Several possibilities will be suggested.

In Chapters 4, 5, and 6, you will get down to the specifics of your changes. You will look at the lunch period in three phases to make it more manageable. Then, you will consider the key aspects of dining behavior and a restaurant-like ambiance. Lots of practical ideas will be presented for how to make improvements.

Chapters 7 and 8 will provide techniques for building excitement for your cafeteria transformation project. You will also learn how to kick off your project with a grand opening day celebration. Ideas for keeping the momentum going will be offered in Chapter 9.

The last chapter of *You Don't Have to Dread Cafeteria Duty* will encourage you to apply to other duties the same kind of creative thinking you are using to transform your cafeteria. This section will make outside recess, hall monitoring, and bus duties more enjoyable for children and adults.

Finally, the Idea Bank in Resource A provides a collection of additional suggestions that you can use to enhance your transformation project. At the end of the book, in Resource B, you will also find reproducible sheets that will make program implementation easier to get started.

## Lots of Help From Our Friends

We would like to thank the many teachers and administrators who were intrigued with the ideas in this book and who tried them out with their students. In addition, we are grateful to the young diners who responded so enthusiastically to the idea of eating in a school restaurant.

Appreciation also goes to Alice Foster, who saw the importance of helping elementary educators cope with the "dreaded duties," and the following colleagues and friends:

- Donald Disney, director of athletics, Howard County School System, Ellicott City, Maryland

- Laurie Feustle, classroom teacher, Carroll County Public Schools, Westminster, Maryland

- Kim Stepherson, physical education teacher, Howard County Public Schools, Ellicott City, Maryland

We would also like to extend our special thanks to Mike Novak and Jerry Wachter.

Finally, our book would not have been possible without the careful work of Marlene Head, who transformed our manuscript into a book to help teachers, administrators, and, most importantly, children enjoy the parts of the school day that are supposed to be refreshing and pleasant.

DORI E. NOVAK
*Columbia, Maryland*

JOANNE C. STROHMER
*Baltimore, Maryland*
*December 1997*

# About the Authors

**Dori E. Novak** is a dynamic educator who has worked in the field of public education for 28 years. She is the Director of Staff Development for the Howard County Public School System in Maryland, where she created and currently manages a nationally recognized staff development and resource center. She also worked as an adjunct instructor at Western Maryland College, where she developed and taught a highly rated course in Creative Classroom Management.

Novak is a keynote speaker, a presenter, and a consultant to education, business, and government groups on classroom management, strategic planning, project design, team building, leadership, risk taking, and mind mapping for creative problem solving. Her clients have included the National Staff Development Council, Goddard Space Flight Center, Griffith Oil Company, Howard County government, National Education Association, Maryland State Department of Education, Loyola College, Mount St. Mary's College, University of Maryland, and a wide array of other professional and private organizations.

She was appointed to the Governor's Commission on Self-Esteem, has authored several nationally published articles, and was elected president of the Maryland Staff Development Council. Novak received her bachelor's degree in Education from the University of Maryland and her master's degree in Science from the Johns Hopkins University. She resides with her husband in Columbia, Maryland.

**Joanne C. Strohmer** has been an educator for more than 20 years. She has taught in both public and private elementary schools. She is currently a supervisor working with elementary, middle school, and high school teachers. In that role, she has a chance to visit many schools and work with teachers and administrators on issues ranging from curriculum to classroom management.

In addition to her work in education, Strohmer's other love is writing. She is the author of more than 50 instructional materials and professional books for teachers. Her most recent work is *Time-Saving Tips for Teachers* (1997, Corwin Press), coauthored with Clare Carhart. Strohmer is currently completing a book on how to get a teaching job.

# 1

# The Dreaded
# School Cafeteria Scene

Close your eyes and think about the cafeteria in your school for a few seconds. Imagine it full of hungry children getting their meals and eating. Not a pretty sight, is it? Chances are your head is full of loud voices, adults' and children's, as you conjure up this scene. The sights you see may be filled with chaotic movement and, perhaps, some less-than-ideal table manners on the part of the young diners. Even the smells your senses are remembering may not be the most appetizing.

Now, take a moment to imagine your cafeteria without the children. Focus on the walls, tables, and floor. Notice the lighting. This is not one of the more pleasant scenes in your school even without the noise and confusion.

## Looking at the Big Picture

It is not uncommon for the school cafeteria to be one of the least favorite sites in the school. Neither children nor adults are usually attracted to spend any more time than necessary in the cafeteria. And the thought of being the adult on duty in the lunchroom can bring even a professional, well-adjusted educator to his or her knees . . . either in surrender or prayer!

We are not asking you to call up these images because we want you to suffer. Rather, if you can think more deeply about the problems with your school cafeteria, you can bring about concrete changes that will make the environment more pleasant for adults and children. If you identify the details that distress you, one by one, you can make improvements in these situations.

## Considering the Details

Think of your lunchroom again, this time in more detail. This can be done alone or in collaboration with colleagues in an informal setting or a faculty and staff meeting. Brainstorm and record your impressions on paper strips or stick-on notes. Consider in detail the pictures that come to mind, the specific noises you hear, and the aromas or odors you smell. Describe the students and what they are doing. Think about how the adults react. Note facial expressions and tone of voice. As you record these ideas, notice how you are feeling doing this task. Label and record those emotions, too.

| | |
|---|---|
| Children using loud voices | Bits of trash on the floor |
| Good food smells | Teacher threatening to keep class in from recess |

Now, sort the strips or notes into positive and negative piles. If there are some items in the positive pile, congratulations to your school! Keep those elements in mind to appreciate and build upon as you work on your cafeteria's image. Carefully consider the pile of negative images and emotions. These are some of your concrete concerns to work on.

## Getting Others Involved in Observing

To heighten awareness and build enthusiasm for a project aimed at improving the cafeteria situation, you might want to involve teachers, staff, parents, and students in taking an objective look at the cafeteria so you can zero in on some areas for improvement. For example, this informal research could be undertaken by the parent-teacher organization, a school improvement team, or a group of talented youngsters.

Some things you and your observers might study are

- The amount of time students spend waiting in cafeteria lines
- The efficiency of serving routines and traffic flow
- Perceptions of treatment of children and staff
- Seating and eating routines
- Dismissal times and procedures
- Lunchroom cleanliness and decor
- Typical student behaviors in the lunchroom

Information about how the cafeteria is currently operating can be gained in a number of ways. For example, a team of a few adults or children might note and record their impressions while the cafeteria is in service. These observations might simply be notes jotted on paper or you might devise a form. (See Resource B, pages 80 to 83, for examples.) Some type of form would be especially useful to schools that are data driven and want to be able to set a baseline and document progress on various indicators.

The more you can describe and quantify what makes the current situation unpleasant, the more likely you will be to take specific steps toward improvement. Those who wish to get creative with their assessment of what currently exists might want to try one or two of the ideas listed in Table 1.1.

After formal or informal means are used to collect information about how the cafeteria now looks, sounds, and feels, these notes should be used as a basis for considering what could be and as a launching pad for creating that new environment. The notes will also be valuable to look back on later to appreciate and celebrate what has been accomplished.

**TABLE 1.1** Some Creative Ways to Look at Your Current Cafeteria

| *What to Use* | *How to Do It* |
|---|---|
| Observational Survey (See Resource B, page 80.) | For several days, a team member can observe in the lunchroom and check off observed behaviors for a clear picture of what exists. |
| Videotape | Portions of various lunch shifts can be taped over a few days for a dramatic picture of what exists. These tapes can be used with the faculty, staff, parents, and children to help them see what currently exists. |
| Anecdotal Records | A committee member or volunteer helper can circulate in the cafeteria and take notes about events, interchanges, and situations during various lunch periods over several days. |
| Time Logs | A team member can log information about arrival and dismissal times for several classes over several days. Some areas for consideration are<br>• Arrival time<br>• Completion of serving and all seated<br>• Beginning of dismissal<br>• Completion of dismissal |
| Behavior Referrals | Information can be tracked about the frequency and nature of behavior problems related to the cafeteria that are directed to the administrators. |
| Surveys (See Resource B, pages 81 to 83.) | Surveys can be distributed to random samples of children, teachers, cafeteria workers, and others who have direct knowledge of the lunchroom. Another version might be devised to collect the perceptions of people who have secondhand impressions, such as parents. |
| Drawings | Children, teachers, and others involved in the cafeteria experience can be asked to show through simple sketches and drawings how they feel about their time in the lunchroom. Of course, the artists should be assured that stick figures are fine. Paints or crayons should be used to convey moods and feelings through colors. |
| Journal Entries | The classroom teacher can invite youngsters to write about the cafeteria in their journals. Sample questions are<br>• How do you feel about eating lunch in our cafeteria?<br>• What are the best and worst things about our school cafeteria?<br>• If you could change three things about our cafeteria, what would they be? |

# 2

# What Could Be

**Picture This**

You and a colleague are following two children down the hall. The youngsters are talking about mutual friends as they walk through the double doors marked "East Side Elementary Restaurant." You turn to your fellow teacher and remark, "I love this little break in the day. It's fun to come in here and chat with the children as they have their lunch."

It seems that from the beginning of public education, teachers and administrators have moaned and groaned about the cafeteria scene. It is almost as though educators have given up and accepted cafeteria chaos as a given. This does not have to be the case, however. Some schools have been successful in establishing a new image for their lunchrooms. In order to create a different kind of cafeteria, the administrators, teachers, and staff of a school have to be able to envision something different from and better than what currently exists. They have to be willing to undertake an attitude adjustment. The first step is to suspend your doubt and experiment with believing that the cafeteria scene can improve, as illustrated in Exhibit 2.1.

---

**Exhibit 2.1: Beliefs**

- Believe that children can learn table and conversational manners.
- Believe that, without spending a lot of money, the cafeteria can be made appealing.
- Believe that you can walk into the lunchroom without getting a knot in your stomach.
- Believe that you can enjoy pleasant interactions with youngsters while they eat their lunch.

---

After all, if your school's lunchroom is like most, it can only get better . . . so what do you have to lose?

Push aside the pangs of disbelief you may be feeling as you read this. Now is a good time to recall that old adage, "Fake it until you make it." What if you and your colleagues made a pact for maybe just a month to talk and act as if you really can transform your lunchroom into a pleasant part of your school?

## Getting a Vision

This chapter will help you design that new image. It will challenge you to imagine your school cafeteria in a new way. For instance, what if you started calling it a school restaurant? This little change in terminology can have a big effect on people's expectations of the lunchroom. The more effort you put into focusing on a clear image of what you would like to see in the future, the more likely you will be to bring about your wish.

As you consider your dreams for how the school restaurant could be, of course, you will think about the kind of ambiance you would like your school's lunchroom to have. You will also consider how you would like the young diners to behave. Do not stop there. Also, ponder how a better daily cafeteria experience could nurture positive self-concepts, affect school climate, and even support academic learning. You can think about these aspects on your own or invite others who work in the school to brainstorm with you.

## Enhancing the Ambiance

Think about the ambiance an ideal school restaurant would have. At this point, do not let the wet blanket part of your mind that we all have limit your fun with this image. Dare to dream big at this stage. Think about what you would like to have if all your wishes could come true.

- What mood would be set in the lunchroom?
- How would seating be arranged or assigned?
- Would a microphone be used? If so, how?
- How could lighting be made pleasant?
- What color would the walls be? What would adorn them?
- How could music be used to enrich the experience?
- How would the traffic flow be managed to maintain the mood?

Another way you could think about the ideal cafeteria is to use a mind map (see Exhibit 2.2) or other visual device to put down your thoughts. Brainstorm about the sights, sounds, smells, and feelings you would like children to experience when they have meals in your school restaurant.

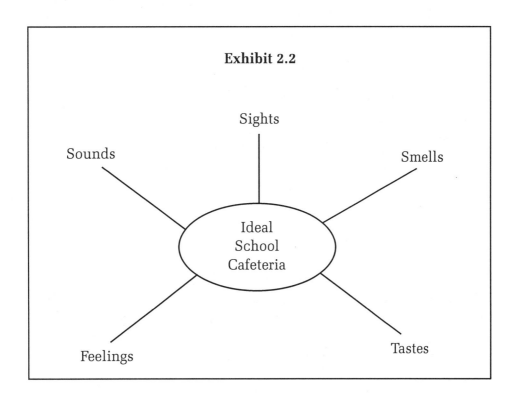

Chapter 6 will provide some more ideas about improving lunchroom atmosphere.

## Polishing Diners' Behaviors

Everyone in the school is affected by how children choose to behave in the cafeteria. The lunchroom offers one of the best times during the school day for youngsters to learn and practice some basic life skills as they engage in an authentic social situation. They have chances to learn and practice

- Self-control as they interact with peers, wait their turns to be served, and handle their emotions and those of others
- Problem solving as they encounter situations such as spills or conflict
- Courtesy and sensitivity in communicating with adults and other diners
- Conversational skills as they talk about interests and problems with peers

Think about how you wish children would behave in the cafeteria. Run a movie in your head of various scenes that would arise during the perfect lunch period. Think about how "award-winning" children would respond in the following typical situations:

- Waiting in line
- Asking cafeteria workers for something
- Talking with friends at the table
- Dealing with disagreements with peers at the table
- Interacting with shy or less popular children
- Handling spills or other accidents
- Cleaning up their areas
- Dealing with dismissal procedures

Consider what kind of responses to these situations would result in a peaceful, pleasant, relaxing lunch break. Once you and your colleagues have a clear picture in your minds of how you would like diners to behave, Chapter 5 will show you how to establish those behaviors in your school's restaurant.

## Nurturing Self-Esteem

The school cafeteria can be dangerous territory for children who are socially unskilled or ones who have special needs. Shy or disabled youngsters may dread the typical lunchroom experience. Modifying the cafeteria environment and putting a schoolwide focus on courtesy, cooperation, and acceptance of diversity can be helpful to the esteem of all youngsters.

Children with positive self-esteem feel like they belong, believe they are worthwhile, and feel able to make significant contributions in many situations. They understand that they have control over their choices and that unsatisfactory results can usually be corrected by making different choices in the future. The school lunchroom can provide a chance for children to become aware of their decision-making skills and practice them in an authentic social environment. Positive self-esteem in the lunchroom setting can lead to feelings of confidence in academic situations. These goals can be supported by establishing positive guidelines and implementing minilessons designed to teach effective social skills. See Chapter 5 for more ideas about how to accomplish this outcome.

## Adding Hundreds of Hours of Learning

Children spend anywhere from 400 to 600 hours, or the equivalent of half a school year, in the cafeteria during the 5 or 6 years of their elementary school careers. In many school systems, youngsters spend more time in the lunchroom than they do in art, music, or physical education classes. Meanwhile, educators frequently lament about the lack of time to cover all they have to teach. They acknowledge the need for children to apply what they learn in meaningful settings and to integrate knowledge and skills, yet they do not generally consider the opportunity available in the form of the daily lunch break. Viewed with new eyes, the cafeteria can provide a gold mine of additional hours of informal, real-life practice of social and academic skills.

If the school is a home away from home for children, the cafeteria is the school family's kitchen. It can be a place to learn and practice good social habits as well as other important peer skills. Historically, young people have learned social skills in their home environment. Because of changes in our economy and family structure, young children frequently miss opportunities to learn conversation skills and manners at family meals. Through the kind of quick activities and reinforcements described in Chapter 5 and the Idea Bank in Resource A, youngsters can acquire some of these behaviors.

Not only can the school's cafeteria provide a "social apprenticeship," but meals can also be a time for children to naturally and informally apply what they are learning in their classrooms. For instance, lunchroom conversation gives children a wonderful opportunity to put communication and thinking skills into action. The lunch period is a break for children and should not be ruined with formal expectations. However, many of the following will occur naturally or can be gently encouraged during lunch breaks.

- Discussion skills such as describing, retelling, elaborating, clarifying, asking and answering questions, and being aware of the audience
- Conversation about books the children are reading
- Collaboration and cooperation

- Problem solving, brainstorming, predicting, decision making, analyzing, and synthesizing

Again, noting these connections between cognitive skills and the school restaurant is *not* meant to imply that youngsters should be sent to eat their meals with a list of assignments to complete. A major thrust of the ideas in this book is to make lunchtime more relaxing. It is possible, however, to use this time to support learning in unobtrusive ways. For example, alerting adults in the lunchroom to be on the lookout for opportunities to compliment individuals on their use of communication, conflict resolution, and thinking skills may be all that is needed.

## Improving School Climate

The cafeteria experience is one that is common and familiar to everyone in your school. Working on a plan to rethink your lunchroom and seeing the results can inspire and unite children, teachers, administrators, family members, cafeteria workers, custodians, and secretaries. Accepting the challenge for making mealtime in the school restaurant an enjoyable and productive experience can promote a sense of community and school spirit for all. Thinking of the lunchroom as a relaxing restaurant may significantly add to a warm, accepting atmosphere in the school. This climate can have a positive effect on self-esteem.

## Getting Started

Once your vision of what could be starts to come into focus, ideas about how to organize a transformation effort will also begin to pop into your mind. For many schools, the stages of the project are predictable. Exhibit 2.3 shows some of the elements your program may include.

A checklist like the one on page 84 may help you keep track of the project steps. The remaining chapters in this book will lead you through the thinking and tasks needed to make your overall plan come alive.

---

**Exhibit 2.3: Overall Plan**

- Identify the specific aspects of your school cafeteria that are not working smoothly and pleasantly at this time.
- Develop a schoolwide philosophy regarding the expectations and desired climate for the school lunchroom.
- Identify who will plan and carry out ideas related to the philosophy and expectations.
- Reach schoolwide consensus on a few important standards for cafeteria behavior.
- Improve the looks, sounds, smells, tastes, and feelings in your school lunchroom.
- Involve everyone who is willing to be a part of transforming your cafeteria.
- Maintain your gains, plan to continue fine-tuning the changes, and celebrate your successes.

---

# 3

# Making the Dream Come True

---

### Picture This

You enter the media center and head for a table where a few teachers,
a custodian, a cafeteria worker, and a couple of upper-grade elementary students are meeting. As you get closer, you hear bits of animated
conversation. "We could ask Ms. Michaels to work with her art class on
a mural for the wall." "Mr. Martin from Martin's Hardware said he would
give us some paint." They see you coming and call out, "Hey, how is
your committee doing on the standards for restaurant behavior?"

---

Y ou have now clearly identified what distresses you about your current cafeteria and started to build a vision of what could be. The next
question is, "Who could make this dream come true?"

## Considering Options

Naturally, as a reader of this book, you would be a logical key player,
but there are various ways you and your colleagues could structure a
project aimed at transforming your school cafeteria into a pleasant restaurant for children. Careful thought about the setup will ensure that

---

**Exhibit 3.1: Three Ways to Implement the Project**

- Hercules Approach

- Pioneer Approach

- Lone Ranger Approach

---

you come up with a practical plan that matches the time and talents of people in your building. Consider some options, as shown in Exhibit 3.1.

Next, look at the advantages and disadvantages of each to see which fits your situation best.

## Hercules Approach

This approach requires one or more brave souls to take on the challenge of coordinating a project involving the whole school. One advantage to this approach is that consistent procedures and standards are developed for the whole school. Therefore, after the initial implementation year, each subsequent year becomes easier to manage as children move from grade to grade with the same behavior expectations and agreements. A likely champion for this broad implementation would be the school's principal, assistant principal, or an active, committed parent volunteer.

### *Other Advantages*

- Excitement can be generated around a theme or schoolwide campaign for the changes.
- Everyone can help implement the program from his or her classroom with the support of every other individual in the school.
- The entire parent-teacher association and community can be tapped for support.
- Strengthening school spirit and staff morale can be a bonus side benefit.

### *Disadvantages*

- Such large-scale change can be hard to manage.

- Everyone may not be eager to participate; therefore, consistency may be a problem and coordinators may need to put extra effort into soliciting and encouraging support.

- Initial implementation mistakes could create schoolwide disruptions. (A small-scale pilot would give everyone a chance to observe, problem solve, and suggest changes before wide-scale implementation is attempted.)

- It may be hard to release schoolwide planning teams to meet regularly to coordinate the implementation.

## Pioneer Approach

This plan calls for a small group of enthusiasts such as the teachers from one lunch shift or grade level who are committed to making their lunch periods more positive experiences for everyone. They might even agree to serve as a pilot for a few months or a year with feedback and support from the whole staff.

### *Advantages*

- The number of people involved in the change effort is smaller.

- It may be easier for the principal to find ways to release small numbers of teachers and others to do the necessary planning.

- The results could be more immediate. A few enthusiastic teachers could get together, plan, and implement the program more quickly without having to convince every teacher in the building to become involved.

- The whole school could keep informed about the progress, be involved in problem solving, and provide support to the risk-taking team. When the success is achieved, it is easier for other teams to follow in the already-cleared path developed by the Pioneering Team.

### *Disadvantages*

- This approach will take longer to spread to the entire school because it is done in smaller chunks.

- Different teams will be in varying stages of implementation.

- The initial pilot team may get more support and attention than subsequent teams.

## Lone Ranger Approach

This approach is recommended for an individual classroom teacher, one or more instructional assistants, a group of parent volunteers, or a combination of these who want to start by making a difference with just one class. This is perhaps the most challenging approach to implement, but it is a viable place to start, especially if support does not yet exist for a larger effort. The positive results will speak for themselves and likely generate more widespread enthusiasm in time.

### *Advantages*

- Children can be more directly involved in developing a plan for their class.
- One class can become the star and a great advertisement for future implementation in the entire school.
- Implementation can proceed faster because fewer decision makers are involved.
- One person has full control over the implementation.

### *Disadvantages*

- It is harder to teach one group of students about new expectations that do not apply to all children in the school.
- Each year, the Lone Ranger will have to establish the program all over again as new children arrive in the fall.
- One person has all the responsibility.

## Forming an Implementation Team

With any luck, one of the three scenarios or a variation will fit your needs. Once basic decisions have been made about the scope of the project, an implementation team and a coordinator need to be identified. These individuals will have a variety of tasks:

- Developing details of the transformation plan
- Seeking approval
- Keeping the staff informed
- Coordinating the kickoff activities
- Monitoring progress
- Solving problems that arise

The number of team members will vary depending on the scope of the project. They will need administrative support in finding times to meet, especially at the beginning of the effort.

## Choosing a Coordinator

With a variety of activities to be undertaken, it is helpful to approach this project as a team effort even if it is to be implemented with just one class at first. In order to keep on track, a leader needs to be chosen for the team. Careful selection of the coordinator is vital to the success of the implementation. One passionate, committed, enthusiastic believer is needed for this role.

The ideal coordinator will be experienced in working with adults, have good communication and public relations skills, and be respected by both students and staff. He or she will need to inspire others to work on planning and implementation. The coordinator will also facilitate communication, encourage participation, and support others in working through the inevitable challenges that arise.

Possible candidates might be the principal, a nonteaching assistant principal, a team leader, or an instructional assistant. Another option is an enthusiastic parent volunteer who can devote a regular and sufficient amount of time to the project. If a team leader or other teacher is going to provide leadership for the project, every effort should be made to give him or her some release time for this endeavor that will have an impact on the school climate.

Once the team and coordinator have been identified, planning meetings will be needed. Two critical agenda items will be (1) deciding on the list of tasks that must be done in order to transform the cafeteria into a pleasant restaurant environment and (2) determining who will do each task. The Action Planning Form on page 85 may be helpful.

## Building a Team Effort

Even though an implementation team and coordinator will be most directly involved with the project, there will be a continuous need for communication with many people from the school and community. Getting cafeteria workers, custodians, assistants, secretaries, parents, volunteers, and community business people excited about and involved in the vision will enhance the effort. The lunchroom is the hub of school-wide interest from late morning until early afternoon. Everyone can play a part in making it a pleasant place that nurtures youngsters.

# 4

# As Simple as 1-2-3:
# Managing the Phases of Lunchtime

## Picture This

You are showing a new parent in your community around the school. You purposely save the best, the school restaurant, for last. As you enter, the settling phase is ending with the last few children finding their seats. Everyone else is chatting at their tables. You stop by the VIP section, where one of the youngsters explains that her class is enjoying the special treat of place mats and a cute centerpiece because they are being recognized for their good restaurant manners. You wish the parent could stay to see how smoothly cleanup and dismissal work, but she has to go back to her job.

Although it may seem like it lasts for hours, most elementary school lunch periods are only about 30 minutes long. The challenge of positively managing that half hour can be immediately simplified by thinking of the lunchtime as having three distinct 10-minute phases, as shown in Exhibit 4.1.

Each phase has its own unique purpose for which specific management strategies and reinforcement activities can be selected.

---

**Exhibit 4.1: Three-Phase Cafeteria Management Plan**

**GET!**   *Phase 1: Settling* (5-10 minutes)
Students arrive in the cafeteria, wait in the serving line, and get settled at tables.

**EAT!**   *Phase 2: Maintenance* (5-10 minutes)
Students eat lunch, interact socially, and stay alert to signals for buying dessert and returning trays.

**GO!**   *Phase 3: Cleanup and dismissal* (5-10 minutes)
Students clean up, line up, and are dismissed from the lunchroom.

---

## Managing the Three Phases of Lunchtime

Carefully considering each phase and its purpose will allow adults to plan for routines that result in a pleasant mealtime. Making these phases and the expectations about each explicit to young diners will support them in acquiring appropriate restaurant behaviors.

### Settling Phase

During the settling phase, the students arrive in the cafeteria and wait in line to be served or take their bag lunches directly to their seating area. In addition to using clear explanations and modeling to teach children what is expected for this phase, simple games and techniques can be used to encourage and support their growth in these behaviors. See the Idea Bank in Resource A for the Gallery Walk and Line Walkers.

These games are both fun and an important part of the student training program. The objective is to set clear expectations and help students establish new habits that will result in a positive, orderly, and enjoyable lunch experience. Once the habits are established, the strategies can be used less and less often. They can then be used from time to time for reinforcement or to remind children if the standards begin to slip.

### Maintenance Phase

As the students are seated, the maintenance phase begins. During this time, the children are eating their lunches, socializing, and looking forward to recess. Often they need to be excused for drinks of water or a chance to use the restroom. A plan needs to be worked out to allow this to happen in an orderly way. It is not acceptable to restrict children's use of the water fountain and restrooms to before or after lunch.

Making sure whatever procedures are instituted are fair and reasonable encourages both children and adults to cooperate and uphold agreements. A system that incorporates the use of passes is helpful. This kind of procedure ensures that only a few children will be out at a time. See the Idea Bank for Clothespin Passes as one example of a management strategy. Other approaches that can be used during the maintenance phase are the Cylinder Game, Lucky Lotto, Videotaped Stars, and VIP Tables found in the Idea Bank in Resource A.

## Cleanup and Dismissal Phase

This final phase is usually the busiest and most challenging of all. The goal is to have children responsibly return their lunch trays to the designated area, dump their trash, and return in an orderly manner to their tables. At this time, posted standards explained in Chapter 5 help make expectations very clear.

Management strategies described in the Idea Bank provide good incentives to students. These include the Roving Photographer and Bulletin Board of the Stars. However, the best incentive is usually the reward of being invited, based on most restaurant-like behavior, to line up first for recess. Once 20 or 30 children are in line, they can be very obviously ushered outside first for recess. Even though this may mean only 2 or 3 extra minutes of play time, it is the ultimate reward for many youngsters.

During this final phase, training strategies including Stop Signs and Line Walkers (from the Settling Phase) can be used. After 2 or 3 weeks of upholding consistent expectations and offering visible rewards for meeting the standards, the behaviors will be routinized and less and less teacher effort will be required. When individual students or classes begin to slip on observing the agreed-upon standards, quick attention should be given in the form of reviewing the original behavior agreements. The survey of seven desired behaviors (see How's It Going? on page 78) can be used to identify the specific behaviors that need attention. Parents can be called on to encourage and support the efforts.

## Planning for the Phases

Thinking of the lunch period in these three phases will simplify the process. You might want to do a little more focused observation now that you have been introduced to this concept. For example, you could use the form on page 86 to organize your thoughts and goals about each of these phases. You can also involve children in self-evaluation if you acquaint them with the three phases. Remember, the more concrete you can be about verbalizing how you would like to see your school restaurant run, the more likely it is that you will be able to transform the vision into reality.

With your goals in mind for each phase of the cafeteria time, you can turn to some specific implementation plans. These will focus around two key issues: (1) defining and nurturing restaurant-like behavior by the diners and the adults helping them and (2) enhancing the lunchroom atmosphere.

# 5

# Teaching Restaurant-Like Behavior

---

**Picture This**

You are on duty in the cafeteria and notice two children who are in a heated discussion at the other side of the room. You hurry over to their table, only to hear another youngster at the table say, "Take it easy, Lee. Jim didn't mean to spill his milk on you." Another child chimes in, "Yeah, people in a restaurant wouldn't act like that. They'd just say 'Excuse me' and clean it up." By the time you get to the table, the youngsters have calmed down, and everyone is sopping up the little bit of milk with paper napkins.

---

In Chapter 1, when you first considered the current status of your school lunchroom, a big part of the "horror" you felt was related to the behaviors of children. In some cases, the demeanor of adults on duty in the cafeteria was also distressing. Identifying the student and adult behaviors that would make the cafeteria a more pleasant place is a major key to success of your cafeteria transformation project. Once you can envision those behaviors, the next step is to communicate and teach them to everyone involved.

> **Exhibit 5.1: Behavior Goals**
>
> *Children:* to behave in a courteous, mature, peaceful way while enjoying their lunch
>
> *Adults:* to interact with "customers" in the school restaurant with courtesy, friendliness, and dignity

## Identifying Broad Goals

Just as some restaurants establish special codes such as "No Smoking" or "Jackets Required," the school staff needs to establish agreements about what will be acceptable in the school restaurant. These agreements are aimed at ensuring that everyone can get maximum enjoyment and relaxation from dining in school.

First, think about the broad goals for behavior. Get some children and adults to work together to verbalize these desired outcomes. For instance, Exhibit 5.1 shows one example of how this might look.

These broad goals might be made into a banner or attractive large poster and placed prominently just outside the cafeteria entrance, much as some restaurants display their mission statement.

## Getting Specific

After the big goals have been decided upon, children and adults can collaborate on establishing agreements about specific behaviors that will support these aims. The standards should be few in number, succinctly stated, and communicated in positive terms. They should be posted inside the cafeteria in a location where they can be easily read by children in their lunchroom seats.

## Deciding on Standards

There are many methods a class, grade, or school can use to arrive at behavior standards for students. For instance, proposed standards can be brainstormed by a committee with a representative from each of the following groups:

- Students
- Teachers
- Administrators

---

**Exhibit 5.2. Example of Restaurant Behavior Expectations**

**Welcome to the Jefferson School Cafe**

*Please*

- Be polite to others.
- Always walk.
- Use conversational voices.
- Leave the area ready for the next person.

*Thank you*

---

- Cafeteria workers
- Custodians

Their work could be presented for input from the school, revised, and turned into a final draft.

Another alternative is for each class that will be involved to work on a list of proposed standards. A committee could then select the best set to be adopted schoolwide (see Exhibit 5.2, for example).

## Establishing Consequences and Rewards

Consequences of not meeting the standards also need to be brainstormed and agreed upon in advance. A committee that includes staff, children, and parents can be challenged to carry out this task. It is important that the focus be on stopping unsafe or inappropriate behavior in a constructive manner that guards the dignity of those involved. Consequences need to be clearly defined, communicated to all school staff as well as parents, and carried out fairly.

Not only do consequences need to be thought out in advance, but serious consideration also needs to be given regarding how youngsters will be recognized and rewarded for growth in learning and applying the standards. This is such an important key to the success of the plan that an entire section of Chapter 9 will be devoted to it.

## Communicating the Standards to All

Once the behavior expectations, consequences, and rewards have been agreed upon, they need to be communicated to staff, students, and parents. The posting of the standards in the school restaurant is one part of being sure everyone is aware of the expectations. Again, students as well as adults can be challenged to use their creativity to find fun ways to let everyone know about the standards. Some possibilities are

- Posters
- Public-address announcements
- Notes on menus
- Skits
- Bookmarks

## Committing to Restaurant Behavior

Regardless of how the guidelines are created, commitment must be sought from all who will be expected to uphold the standards. An effective way to do this is to use a Consensus Mural. This mural can be a student-created artwork that illustrates the new image of the school restaurant and also incorporates the standards. The mural can be a painting, drawing, or magazine picture collage. The art teacher might be invited to be a consultant or coordinator for this part of the project.

After it is completed, all children can be given a chance to sign the mural as a symbol of their participation in improving their lunchroom. The resulting art can be displayed on a wall in the restaurant.

Another option is to create individual contract forms that state the guidelines for restaurant behavior. Each child can be invited to sign a contract.

## Teaching Restaurant Behavior

In order for children to be successful in learning restaurant-like behaviors, they must understand what is involved and how to implement the standards. For example, although the meaning of "using conversational voices" may be perfectly clear to adults, this concept needs to be taught to children. You cannot assume youngsters magically know how to behave in a restaurant without instruction any more than you can assume they are born with a knowledge of how to do long division without careful teaching of the steps and conventions involved.

Five- or 10-minute minilessons on the new standards will help children get a clear picture of the expectations. The Minilesson Frame on page 87 provides a planning frame for creating these lessons. This instruction can help children become aware that their behavior is always their choice. Each desired outcome can be reinforced with repeated minilessons on the same topic so that lasting learning occurs.

These lessons are not meant to be squeezed into an already crowded curriculum. They can be presented in the cafeteria during lunchtime for several days in preparation for the transformation of the cafeteria into a more restaurant-like atmosphere. Other options include using the lessons for "fillers" at the beginning or end of the day, before or after lunch, or during transition times. Some topics for minilessons include

- Using conversational voices in the lunchroom and hallways
- Waiting in line
- Respectfully interacting with cafeteria workers and other adults
- Politely asking for something while at the table
- Telling about an incident (use of retelling skills in a social setting)
- Taking turns in conversation
- Disagreeing respectfully with what someone has said
- Managing peer pressure
- Resolving conflict without using physical force
- Using appropriate language

As students and adults work on determining the broad goals for behavior and specific expectations, many other potential topics for minilessons will arise. It is easy to see how taking a few moments here and there to teach these behaviors will make not only lunchtime but other times more pleasant and easy to manage as youngsters learn to be courteous and considerate.

## Viewing Adults as Hosts in the Restaurant

Pleasant child-to-child and child-to-adult interactions need to be nurtured for the cafeteria to become a pleasant place. Also, adult-to-child interactions are crucial for setting a new tone.

In the frustration of trying to deal with a mass of exuberant youngsters at lunchtime, it is easy to take on a drill sergeant role. However, if the cafeteria is to be transformed into a school restaurant, not only must children learn to use restaurant manners and social skills, but adults also need to start thinking of themselves as gracious hosts in the restaurant. It is worthwhile for cafeteria workers, custodians, teachers, administrators, and assistants on duty in the cafeteria to have some discussions of how this would look. Formal or informal goals for the adults involved can result from these conversations.

You may be starting to doubt the feasibility of having children and adults cooperate to implement these new attitudes and behaviors. Remember, however, that this change will unfold as a process and not a dramatic overnight transformation. Realistically, there will be times when the standards are not met by individual children. At those points, positive action must be taken quickly to help youngsters get back on track.

# 6

# Deciding Decor:
# From Institutional Blah
# to Affordable Pizzazz

---

### Picture This

You walk down the hall and turn left at the sign that says "Elm Elementary Restaurant: The Fun Place to Eat." Lunchtime has not yet started, so the room is empty except for cafeteria workers bustling around. You marvel at how different the room looks from just a month ago. The walls are decorated with large colorful posters done by the school's best artists. Even though there are no windows, the room is bright and cheerful with soft light. Fingerpainted place mats created by first graders catch your eye. And then you notice some background music. Nice touch! The restaurant committee always has another creative idea for making lunchtime relaxing.

---

Working on the ambiance of the school restaurant is an aspect of the transformation project that will arouse the enthusiasm and imagination of adults and children in the school as well as community supporters. Let as many people as possible become involved, even if in small ways. There is plenty to be done. The transformation of the lunchroom environment can involve the following:

- Themes
- Sights
- Tastes and smells
- Sounds
- Feelings

The implementation committee will find that it is easy and fun to brainstorm decor ideas. This chapter includes some possibilities to get you started.

## Themes

Before you discuss the details of your lunchroom decor, you might want to consider choosing a theme. Think about some restaurants that cater to children. They use settings, colors, and characters that appeal to youngsters. You might want to do the same. For example, following are some possible themes:

- Jungle
- Underwater world
- Circus
- Favorite cartoon characters
- Time period such as the Old West
- Sport or activity children enjoy

In addition to selecting a theme, decide whether you plan to use this theme for an indefinite period of time or whether you intend to change the decor from year to year or season to season. This decision will have an effect on whether or not you will make permanent changes such as painting scenes on the wall.

The method used for choosing a theme can be a way to build interest and ownership in the project. For instance, individuals or classes could be asked to enter a contest to determine a theme. If the theme is to be changed during the course of the year, certain grades or classes could be responsible for selecting and implementing themes on a monthly or quarterly basis.

Once you have established a theme, you can enjoy considering how details of the decor will help you carry it out. The whole school neighborhood can get involved in figuring out how to implement the theme.

## Sights

You can have great fun playing with what youngsters see as they enter their new restaurant. Get their help in brainstorming possibilities by asking them to draw or write journal entries about their dream lunchroom. You may not be able to accommodate all their wishes, but you can experiment with lighting, wall color, wall hangings, and other accessories to create a brand-new look based on what they like.

## Lighting

One change that can immediately have a major impact on the lunchroom atmosphere is altering the lighting. Most school cafeterias have glaring light. Softening the lighting can make the atmosphere more like a restaurant. Try one of these options:

- Turn off every other row of lights.
- Install dimmer switches.
- Replace one third of the lights with soft-light fluorescents.

Of course, you do not want the lighting to be too dim, just a little softer. Not only will this alteration improve the looks of the lunchroom, it may also support the goal of good restaurant behavior. Some studies have found a correlation between harsh lighting and increased hyperactivity.

## Wall Color

Another big improvement can be brought about by changing the wall color. Instead of an institutional-looking hue, imagine how the room would appear with a soft, warm color. A light yellow or very pale rose will make the room inviting and also make it appear a little smaller and cozier.

It may be hard to convince the district office to repaint your lunchroom if the current paint job is in good repair. Consider a creative solution such as a Saturday parent painting party. Perhaps a local hardware store would donate paint if a plaque with the store's name were displayed in the school restaurant or if local media were on hand to report the event. Another option is to hold a creative fundraiser, such as asking parents to donate the cost of a quart or a gallon of paint. Special badges or bumper stickers could be made to thank the donors.

## Wall Hangings

Most school cafeterias have dull, haphazard wall decorations. By planning out wall areas, you can dramatically improve the visual interest of your lunchroom.

Try to think like an interior decorator. Better yet, see if one of the parents in your school has design training. See if he or she would be willing to spend an hour with the implementation team to look at the lunchroom and brainstorm possibilities.

Decorators do not randomly hang pictures and posters. They look at each area and create groupings that fit the size, shape, and function of the space. If your cafeteria is like most, it has lots of available wall space. You might consider some of the following to add interest to various wall spaces:

- Permanent mural painted on the wall
- Temporary mural or collage on a giant piece of paper
- Gallery of children's art matted and/or framed with construction paper or tagboard
- Groupings of posters related to the lunchroom decor theme
- Artwork on display from the local middle or high school
- Changing exhibits of paintings, photos, or drawings by talented faculty, staff, and parents

If the lunchroom ceiling is very high, you might also want to look up as you consider decor. Mobiles or hanging banners can bring the ceiling down and make the space cozier. These art pieces should hang well and not be flimsy, off balance, or curling. It might be worthwhile to contact neighborhood high school art teachers to see if some classes might take on the challenge of designing and creating decorations to hang from the ceiling.

Whether the school has decided to have changing themes or an on-going theme, it is important to replace at least some of the wall decor periodically. Being greeted by new sights from time to time will help keep interest in the school restaurant alive.

## Other Accessories

An infinite number of other small decor details can be added to make the lunchroom inviting and restaurant-like. For instance, plants can soften the atmosphere. Inexpensive real or silk greens are pleasant additions.

Local businesses that sell plants might be willing to make donations from time to time, as might parents. Also, if the district vocational or science program includes horticulture, the local high school might be interested in taking on the project of supplying live green or flowering plants. The tending of the plants could be one of the jobs of the Restaurant Helpers as described on page 73.

Let your imagination run wild with other special touches:

- Place mats made by children in the school
- Inexpensive vinyl tablecloths to designate special tables
- Holiday or other decorative paper napkins
- Child-made or inexpensive centerpieces

Many of these decorator touches such as centerpieces can be purchased over time and used on a rotating basis from year to year. Some can be bought inexpensively at dollar stores, wholesale clubs, or yard sales. Also, senior citizens' centers often are looking for enjoyable projects to do and may be willing to form a partnership with the school. In most cases, parents, community members, and local businesses will be glad to join the fun of transforming the cafeteria by donating small items.

All of the accessories do not have to be used all of the time. As a matter of fact, it will be more effective if the touches are sprinkled throughout the year so that something new and surprising will always be happening in the school restaurant.

## Tastes and Smells

Ironically, changing the foods offered in the school restaurant is the most difficult area to tackle. In reality, there is not much flexibility in what can be offered. Most of the transformation effort will be spent on the setting in which children eat rather than on what they actually eat.

The implementation committee members can challenge themselves, however, to see what creative innovations they can devise. For instance, children will appreciate and enjoy efforts put into naming the dishes. What menu items are called may relate to the restaurant's theme or to an upcoming holiday.

Also, local businesses may be willing to make donations for special occasions. For example, a grocery store might be able to donate a treat for those celebrating a birthday as part of the festivities described in Happy Birthday to You in the Idea Bank. They may also be willing to furnish an occasional surprise like a lollipop for each diner. Of course, whenever community members support the efforts of the school restaurant, their generosity should be appreciated personally and publicly through thank-you notes, mentions in the school newsletter, and if possible, media attention.

## Sounds

Sounds in the school restaurant can also enhance the lunch experience. One aspect concerning sounds related to conversation can be addressed by teaching restaurant manners as described in Chapter 5. Other opportunities to experiment with the effect of sounds involve providing background music and entertainment.

# Background Music

Music can improve the ambiance in a school lunchroom. Think about how background music in a restaurant affects you. Sitting at a nice table listening to soothing music can help you slow down and relax. On the other hand, blaring music in a trendy bar can supercharge the atmosphere. Considering the natural energy level of a roomful of elementary children, you probably want to aim for the soothing effect and save the supercharge for the playground.

Soft background music can make the eating experience a little calmer. Instrumental music works best. Experiment with the following:

- Very light classical pieces
- Mood music with nature sounds
- Movie theme selections or show tunes

In addition to background music, you might consider selecting three different pieces of music to accompany the three phases of the lunch period. Another variation is to play certain pieces to signal the start of certain activities such as time to get ice cream. A side benefit of this use of music is that it can decrease microphone use to some extent. See Microphone Manners on page 77 to get other ideas about how to judiciously use this tool so it does not cause sound pollution.

The implementation committee can select and try out several kinds of music to determine which types work best to establish the desired mood and signal activities. A parent volunteer group might also find this task fun and challenging. It may be a good idea to have a volunteer act as an observer when a new kind of music is being tried to focus specifically on its effect.

Another possibility is to get youngsters involved in selecting music. The idea is not to have youngsters simply choose their favorite popular pieces. Rather, the situation presents a perfect opportunity for them to use critical thinking to study various kinds of music.

The music teacher or a knowledgeable volunteer can help a group of children consider the type of atmosphere the school is aiming for in the restaurant. They can listen to various pieces, note how they feel, and predict the effect in the lunchroom. Youngsters can also be challenged to notice the kinds of music they hear in restaurants and stores and observe its effect on them. Those involved in selections can then monitor the results and interview their peers about how various pieces played in the school restaurant make them feel.

In addition to background music, musical performances and other types of entertainment can be used to support or reward restaurant behavior. Occasional programs can provide variety and a positive focus.

## Entertainment

Although you will not want to overdo lunchtime entertainment because part of the fun is having time to talk with friends, occasional programs can add to the atmosphere. Occasionally, you might want to consider treating the children to musical programs. These could be performed by groups from your school, musicians from neighboring middle or high schools, or community performers who are willing to donate their talent.

If you select outside performers, be sure you or someone whose judgment you trust has heard the performer or groups and that the music and style of delivery are ones that will appeal to children. If the program is one that requires quiet attention, as opposed to providing background music, it should be kept short so youngsters still have some time to socialize.

Other kinds of performances could also fit into your restaurant project. For instance, short skits by people from within or outside the school, storytelling, or read-alouds for part of Phase 2 can be arranged. See Featuring Live Entertainment on page 76 for more possibilities.

Background music as well as more structured programs can have a positive effect on diners' feelings about their lunch experience. There are other innovations that can also build positive feelings in youngsters who eat in the school restaurant.

## Feelings

In addition to providing children a lunch place that appeals to their senses, you want to be sure the restaurant is emotionally appealing as well. It is important that children finish their lunch break with positive feelings and a readiness for a pleasant and productive afternoon of learning. Many of the ideas in the chapters and the Idea Bank support this goal. Following are a few other suggestions you might also explore.

Traffic patterns can be one focus of your exploration. Diners do not feel good when they are jostled and crunched as they move around and wait in line. When you were surveying your current situation, you probably examined traffic patterns. Now, think how you could improve this aspect.

You might want to draw up a diagram of your lunchroom and challenge some youngsters who are skilled with spatial concepts to brainstorm various traffic pattern options. You could also determine whether this task fits in with the math curriculum at any grade level and see if teachers want to pursue this challenge as a real-life project. Once some ideas are generated, they can be discussed and the most promising ones tried out and analyzed to see whether they improve the feelings of the patrons.

A major way to support positive feelings among restaurant diners is to consider how "support" people can make the experience of eating lunch at school a low-stress experience. The idea of the adults on duty thinking of themselves as gracious hosts has already been mentioned. This tone can be set using simple practices such as greeting and welcoming children as they enter the restaurant.

Considering that the adult on duty has many demands on him or her during a lunch period, you might also consider innovative ways to include "assistant hosts" in your program. For instance, older children might be given a brief training session in how they could help with problems such as getting children items they forgot to get when going through the line or assisting diners in cleaning up spills. Parent or community volunteers might also be willing to serve in this role, considering that your lunchroom will now be a pleasant place in which to spend a half hour or so.

You might also think about including a customer service table in your lunchroom. This table could be a well-marked and pleasantly decorated table that is clearly visible and accessible but out of the main traffic pattern. This can be a temporary refuge where children might go if they experience a problem or have a concern. It could be staffed by a volunteer who would help the child solve his or her problem and get back to the lunch table. If a particular diner is having a hard time at his or her table and needs another place to be for a few minutes to regain composure, sitting down with the "customer service" helper for a few minutes might help.

In general, the customer service table can provide a positive alternative to a child who is distressed. Rather than act out, he or she can get some support.

## Your Turn

This chapter has presented some ideas about adding pizzazz to your lunchroom. Now it is time for you and your committee to enjoy the fun of brainstorming ideas that would delight your young diners and support them in wanting to make the lunch experience a treat for all.

# 7

# Building Excitement for the Project

## Picture This

Several parents have been working in the school today. At the end of the afternoon, you see them approach you as you work at your desk. One who is always bubbling with ideas speaks first. "We have heard that you are trying to turn the cafeteria into a school restaurant. What a great idea!" Another parent chimes in. "We've been talking about ways we can help." They all start talking at once. You catch phrases here and there like "hold a fundraiser" and "call Margie to see if she will help with decorating ideas." You hold up your arms, laughing, and say, "This is great! But let's hear one idea at a time!"

For the cafeteria transformation project to be most successful, everyone in the school community needs to be informed about key elements of the endeavor. These include the following:

- Description and scope of the plans
- The reasons for the undertaking
- Who is involved
- What expectations will be
- When the project will begin

Adults and children need to feel involved. This goal warrants an exciting promotion campaign. The first step is to get the support and commitment of key players. The second is to generate enthusiasm for the project and build toward an exciting "opening day" celebration.

## Getting Administrative Approval

Because the principal is responsible for all aspects of the school's program, his or her approval is a prerequisite to beginning the transformation. If the principal is not the originator of the idea, you need to present the proposal of a cafeteria transformation to him or her and possibly to the school's leadership team.

The goal is to not only get approval but also stir up enthusiasm and commitment for the exciting project. Most school principals will think they have died and gone to heaven when being presented with such a creative dream by staff members who are willing to help make it come true.

The meeting with the principal and other leadership of the school needs to have the following results:

- The principal has been informed at least about the broad concept and any ideas that have been discussed in preliminary brainstorming.
- The principal has given the "go ahead" for working on this endeavor.
- A time has been set for presenting the concept to faculty and staff that would be involved and interested. (Even if only one team or grade will try out the idea initially, the whole school needs to know about it.)

With the administrator's okay, the project can start unfolding. At this point, faculty and staff can be informed and start to get involved.

## Involving Faculty and Staff Members

The teachers, custodians, assistants, cafeteria workers, secretaries, and any other workers in the school need to be invited to be part of the excitement. Even if only a percentage of the adults in the school will be called on to plan the transformation, everyone should be encouraged to provide initial and ongoing input. This aspect is especially important relative to creating the vision and developing the action plan.

In addition to being involved in the fun of creating a dream of a better way, all faculty and staff members need to be called on for some serious commitments even if they will not actively serve on the implementation team. In order for the project to succeed, everyone needs to agree on and commit to the following key responsibilities:

- Explicitly teaching restaurant behaviors to children who will be involved

- Holding youngsters accountable for the agreed-upon restaurant behavior standards

- Treating children who dine in the lunchroom as valued school restaurant "customers"

## Gaining Children's Enthusiastic Commitment

Children can be involved in many aspects of promoting the "opening" of the school restaurant. Promotional activities will not only build excitement for the project but also give youngsters authentic opportunities to use language arts skills such as writing and public speaking. For instance, youngsters can participate in activities such as

- Writing press releases to let the local newspaper know about the cafeteria transformation

- Creating articles for the school newsletter

- Designing ads and notices for the school menu

- Writing and performing short skits related to restaurant behaviors

- Conducting a contest to name the school restaurant

- Writing letters to local businesses asking for support

- Creating posters related to "opening" day and to restaurant behaviors

- Designing bulletin board displays related to the "new" restaurant

- Producing certificates to reward children for learning the behavior standards

- Taking pictures to promote the new lunchroom and behavior standards and writing captions for them. Videos could also be effective.

See pages 89 and 90 for examples of some ways children can be involved in promoting the new restaurant. You might want to share some of them with youngsters as a way of sparking their own creative ideas.

## Encouraging Parent Participation

As with all school endeavors, parent input and participation is a key to success. It would be a wonderful benefit to have one or more parents on the planning and implementation team. Even parents who cannot be involved in this way need to know about the school's plan for cafeteria transformation. Through parent-teacher organization presentations, menu notices, school newsletters, and other communications, they can be made aware of the school's efforts to make lunchtime more pleasant.

Many will be particularly excited about the focus on restaurant manners. If they are furnished with specific information, they may be willing to reinforce the behaviors at home meals and may be able to participate in some of the programs and celebrations described in the Idea Bank.

## Inviting Community Interest

It is in the community's best interest to support the school in its efforts to not only foster academic success but also nurture young people who will act in a considerate, courteous way when they are out in the community. When local groups and businesses hear about your efforts to transform the school cafeteria into a pleasant restaurant where youngsters can practice social graces, they may get excited about supporting your efforts. Some may be willing to provide funds, services, or goods, such as the following:

- Decorator items such as plants, paint, posters
- Lunchtime entertainment such as music or demonstrations
- Speakers such as people with advertising expertise to talk to children who are working on promotional ideas
- Gift certificates for pizzas, burgers, sodas, or other treats from local restaurants

Get children involved in contacting community members for support. You might want to duplicate the letter on page 91 to provide a model for children who are involved in drafting a letter to a local business.

## Ongoing Support

The patience and ongoing support of administrators, colleagues, and community members while undertaking the challenge of transforming the cafeteria are crucial. Gradually, the agreed-upon changes will become routines. However, this will only happen with persistence and consistent effort. It is important to solicit excitement for the project right at the beginning so that support will be strong when the implementers hit the inevitable little bumps in the road that occur with any endeavor. This effort to build enthusiasm will pay off in at least two ways. Not only will the cafeteria get a new look and feel, but the results of such a collaborative effort can breathe new life into an existing school or get a new school off to a great start.

# 8

# Grand Opening

## Picture This

You are on hall duty and take special note of a boy and a girl who are chattering away as they head for their afternoon buses. You hear the girl say, "I can't wait for tomorrow. The grand opening of our restaurant is going to be fun!" The boy responds, "Yeah, my teacher says we are going to learn the Cylinder Game, and there will be prizes." "Well, I heard we are also going to have surprise visitors and extra treats," the girl adds. As they go their separate ways to get on their buses, the boy calls out, "See you at the grand opening!"

A special event or set of events to initiate the new restaurant concept is an additional way to build excitement and enthusiasm for the transformation of the school cafeteria. Even though in most cases the changes will have to be phased in over time, it is important to establish a particular date as the "grand opening" celebration. This idea will draw attention to the new routines and expectations. It will also give many people a chance to be involved in many creative ways.

# Scheduling

It is important to schedule the "grand opening" after a break or at least a weekend when school personnel and volunteer helpers can make some of the physical changes so the restaurant will look different from the old cafeteria. This approach will make people say, "Something new is happening here." It will be easier to convince youngsters to behave differently if the environment is at least somewhat different.

# Activities

The grand opening should include as much fanfare as you can create. Special events might be scheduled for a week or two to lead up to the celebration of the opening. In addition to school personnel, parents and local businesses should be asked to participate. Consider selecting some of the following ideas:

- Give out opening-day lottery tickets. Select numbers and award prizes to the lucky ticket holders.
- Have cafeteria "hosts" and other lunchroom workers wear T-shirts or hats made specially for the occasion.
- Give corsages or boutonnieres to cafeteria workers.
- Decorate with balloons and streamers.
- Arrange to have something special on the menu.
- Have live music by a school group or someone from the community.
- Invite reporters from local papers.
- Invite central office "dignitaries" and prominent people from the community.
- Record the event with photographs. Use a Polaroid camera, if possible, so the results can be displayed immediately.
- Invite a surprise guest such as a clown or seasonal character.
- Conduct a ribbon-cutting ceremony.
- Have special place mats and centerpieces created by the children.
- Invite children to dress up for the occasion.
- Send personal invitations to anyone from the community who helped with the transformation to attend the grand opening.

# Success With the New Standards

An extremely important aspect of the opening day is that children experience success with the new restaurant behavior standards. It is crucial that they start with a good precedent on that day and see some improvement in the feel of the lunchroom experience even if they slip a bit on subsequent days.

Improved behavior on the opening day can be a challenge, not only because the standards are asking something new of the children but also because the excitement of the festivities may make self-control harder. One way to highlight restaurant behavior on this special day is to use the Consensus Mural described in Chapter 5. The signing of the mural could take place on the morning of the grand opening. Every class can be given a few minutes for each child to put his or her signature of agreement on the artwork. Before the first lunch shift, the mural can be secured to a wall in the restaurant where it will be seen by all. It can even be covered and then "unveiled" at the beginning of each lunch shift on that day to bring dramatic attention to the schoolwide commitment to uphold new standards.

A couple of other steps can be taken to support success on the special day.

- Be sure that youngsters are very clear on expectations as a result of a series of minilessons as described in Chapter 5.

- Find ways to have extra adults on hand this first day to provide support and positive reinforcement. For instance, parents might be invited to join their youngsters or teachers might be asked just for that day to be part of the celebration by having lunch at the children's tables with them.

Another way to support children in being successful restaurant patrons on the grand opening is to schedule the most exciting parts of the celebration for after lunch. Those festivities can be used as a way of recognizing and celebrating the children's good start as mature school restaurant patrons.

## Just the Beginning

A lot of creative thinking, teaching of new standards, refurbishing the lunchroom atmosphere, and collaboration go into getting to the point of the grand opening. This event is, however, just the beginning of an exciting time for any school that undertakes a cafeteria transformation. Not only are more pleasant lunch periods ahead, but also delightful and powerful feelings of having a vision and making it come true.

# 9

# Maintaining and Celebrating Accomplishments

**Picture This**

It is the morning of an inservice training day. The students are at home while you and your colleagues are spending the day in professional activities. You and the others in your building have been asked to report to the cafeteria for your first meeting. As you open the door to the lunchroom, your senses are surprised by what you encounter. Tables in one cozy corner of the room have been set with tablecloths and fresh-cut flowers. Soft classical music is playing. But best of all, heavenly brunch food smells greet you. Then you notice a giant banner hanging by the set tables. It says "Congratulations on the 6-month anniversary of the Eastcliff Elementary Cafe. Thanks for all of your hard work."

It will be comparatively easy to generate enthusiasm for your cafeteria transformation. You need only get past the initial skepticism about whether things can be different from the way they have always been. Then, once you have captured people's imaginations about what could be, you will be off and running. The gala opening celebration will be icing on the cake.

## Keeping the Momentum Going

The challenge will be in maintaining and building upon your accomplishments. Regular spot checks, feedback, and acknowledgment of small and large successes will help maintain the energy and commitment of children and adults. A continuous flow of encouragement during implementation and beyond is a dependable energizer.

## Checking on Progress

In order to know what to celebrate and what to work on fine-tuning, the implementation team will need to train themselves to be careful observers in order to monitor progress and set new goals. The team can decide on a schedule of checkpoints. At these points, adults or upper-grade children will observe and record information about how the program is working. Their notes can then be discussed with the implementation team. Observers can use some of the ideas from Chapter 2 to collect information and compare the current ambiance and behaviors in the school restaurant to their earlier notes about the original cafeteria.

## Appreciating All

Collecting periodic information about how various elements of the school restaurant are operating should provide plenty of ideas about people and accomplishments to celebrate. This appreciation needs to be extended to everyone involved in the project: administrators, teachers, cafeteria workers and custodians, children, and parents and other community members. The project can only be successful with the ongoing cooperation of key people in all groups.

### Administrators

It is important to remember that the transformation of the cafeteria into a school restaurant would never get off the ground without the "go ahead" of the administration. A brave principal has to leap out in faith and say "Yes" in order for there to be a chance for a school's dream of a better lunch experience to come true. Therefore, it is important to recognize and show appreciation for this key role. Naturally, the planning committee will thank the principal when the initial permission to try the project is given. However, it is also important to let the administrator know from time to time that this contribution has not been forgotten. For instance, whenever the program receives accolades from impressed outsiders, it would be natural to note the principal's support.

Also, keep in mind that principals and assistant principals often spend their days immersed in problems and crises. That is just the nature of the job. With this in mind, you might consider being very diligent about remembering to share small and large cafeteria successes with the administrators. Some of these ideas might work for you:

- Take a photo of something that is working particularly well in the "new" lunchroom and give it to the principal. Use a Polaroid camera if one is available so you can share the accomplishment soon after you notice it.
- Encourage children to send notes to the principal and assistant principal about the improvements they are noticing in the lunchroom. They could also draw pictures or write poems about the school restaurant.
- Take a few moments to invite the administrator to stop by the restaurant to see a special program.
- Ask the administrator to stop by the restaurant to notice how well a new routine is being implemented.
- Whenever you hear a positive comment about the cafeteria innovations from an adult or a child, pass it along to the administrator.

Remember that these ideas are not just for the beginning of the project but should be sprinkled throughout the year to keep the energy for the program flowing.

## Teachers

It is very likely that teachers not only will be key players on the planning and implementation committee but will also be very involved in teaching and monitoring youngsters' new restaurant behaviors. As with any school innovation, teachers are crucial to the success of the project. It is important to avoid taking their efforts for granted by providing ongoing recognition and support for the energy and creativity they are contributing.

The following are some ways that you might consider recognizing teacher involvement:

- Plan a sneak preview party in the "new" restaurant before the grand opening. In subsequent weeks and months, use the restaurant as the setting for update meetings. Locate the meeting tables in a cozy nook and include special snacks to help establish the idea of the restaurant as a pleasant place.
- Ask the administrator to take a few moments to recognize the general efforts of all faculty in making positive changes to the lunch environment. People who have made special contributions can also be given a word of thanks, a certificate of appreciation, a small gift, or a card.

- Use a bulletin board in the faculty room as a restaurant appreciation space. Put up notes thanking individual teachers for specific contributions to the project. Be sure that everyone is recognized for some effort, large or small, over time. If someone has not taken the initiative to make a contribution, ask him or her to do some small task and then recognize that on the board.

- Ask the principal or implementation committee to write brief notes to teachers complimenting them on specific accomplishments by their classes when eating in the school restaurant.

Also, recognize that teachers feel proud when individual children within their classes receive recognition for restaurant accomplishments. Be sure to note which teacher works with these youngsters when they are honored for learning restaurant behavior or making contributions to the ambiance of the lunchroom.

## Cafeteria Workers and Custodians

These important members of the school community are often the unsung heroes. The restaurant project gives the school an opportunity to take note of their contributions. Without the cooperation of the cafeteria workers and custodians, improvements to the sights, sounds, smells, tastes, and feelings in the lunchroom would be impossible to achieve and maintain. Following are some ways of recognizing their contributions:

- Highlight individual cafeteria workers and custodians on a bulletin board or newsletter. By telling something about the person and his or her interests and contributions to the project, children and adults will be more likely to take time for individual expressions of appreciation.

- Set aside a few special days during the year to honor the cafeteria and custodian workers. Special decorations, programs, and little presents can be used to express gratitude for their contributions to the success of the project.

Don't forget to also include representatives from these staff groups in ongoing input, planning, and implementation groups. Their perspective will add to the creativity and practicality of plans for continued improvement.

## Children

The cooperation of the restaurant "patrons" is the basis for success of the entire transformation project. It is important to reward initial attempts at the new behaviors children are being asked to acquire. It is just as crucial to continue to recognize and support their efforts as the weeks and months go by. Following are a few ideas for showing children that you appreciate their new mature behaviors:

- Give deserving children stickers or badges with a saying such as Super Diner to recognize their growth in restaurant manners.

- Send appreciation notes or postcards home to families.

- Ask the principal, assistant principal, or another "dignitary" in the school to personally visit classes that are making progress in learning restaurant behaviors. Ask him or her to express appreciation and also give a mini–pep talk about continued growth.

- Rotate bouquets of Mylar congratulations balloons among classes that are doing a good job in the restaurant.

See the Idea Bank for many other ways to show appreciation to children as they make progress in learning restaurant skills.

## Parents and Community Members

The energy and efforts of parents, community members, and business members can greatly enhance a cafeteria transformation project. These people do not *have* to contribute, and therefore the fact that they choose to should not go unrewarded. Appreciation of volunteer efforts is a crucial element of a successful project. Here are some ways to recognize and show gratitude to them:

- Have classes write personal thank-you notes to parents, other volunteers, and local businesses who support the program.

- Periodically hold special programs to honor contributors and volunteers. This recognition could take place in an assembly or as a special program during lunchtime.

- List volunteers and their contributions in the school newsletter.

- Put up a banner in the school to thank volunteers who are working on the lunchroom endeavor.

- Set aside a special table in the school restaurant and invite contributors to enjoy lunch there when they visit the school.

## Focus on Success

As students and staff work on this transformation, it is likely that there will be inevitable rough spots. This is a natural part of any complex project. It is important to avoid the trap of thinking that rough spots, slow results, or missed deadlines mean failure.

Handle what is going wrong as quickly as possible and keep your eyes focused on the vision. Be on the lookout for small successes to celebrate on a regular basis. Appreciation and celebration are the fuel that keeps a successful project moving forward.

# 10

# Managing
# "Other Duties as Assigned"

---

**I. Outdoor Recess**

**II. Hall Monitoring**

**III. Bus Duty**

---

## I. Outdoor Recess

Picture this: One hundred or more exuberant children are having a great time playing in a very active school yard. A closer look reveals a wide variety of activities including play on equipment (swings, slides, climbers, etc.). A blacktopped area is painted with lines for hard-court games like dodgeball, hopscotch, jump rope, volleyball, and basketball. A field area is being used for soccer and softball. A large container near the door holds balls, jump ropes, and other play equipment. (So far, this is a pretty common scene.)

Now, add to the picture: Two active adult recess monitors who see their jobs more as "field coaches" than duty monitors. Students can easily find them on the playground because they are wearing red, easy-to-spot bibs over their jackets. Equipped with whistles, clipboards, and games booklets, they are actively involved in the children's activities and continuously observe the entire playground scene. The monitors are circulating, talking to students, supporting students who haven't been included, suggesting play ideas, applauding, participating, cheerleading, encouraging, but never "parking" for very long in any one place. An outside observer might also notice that the monitors are walking in a "crablike" fashion, moving backwards, forward, and side-to-side around the entire perimeter of the playground. They rarely turn their backs on the children.

Finally, imagine this: A burst of two quick notes from a playground monitor's whistle signals a concern. The sound also reminds all the students that they are being continuously monitored for safe and fair play. The monitor and student get together to discuss the concern. A couple of park-like benches are available for conferring with students, comforting someone, or providing a safe "time-out" spot for students who need to rest or get away for a few minutes to regain their self-control. Students seldom remain at the benches for more than 5 minutes, and the monitors rarely sit there or anywhere else. They know the two secrets for safe playtime are (1) constantly circulate and (2) supervise, supervise, supervise!

## Making Recess Time Easier to Manage

A great recess time does not automatically occur every day in any school! Providing students with a smooth-running, fun-filled, and safe daily playtime requires advance work and carefully planned communication to all school staff, monitors, students, parents, and school volunteers.

As with effective cafeteria management, everyone involved in playground supervision needs to be informed, in writing, of the agreed-upon standards for behavior and playground rules. Standards should be limited to a short list of statements that are positively expressed and stated in kids' language. Typical agreements that lead to a fun-filled and safe recess time include these four basic behavior standards:

1. Practice self-control.
2. Always try your best.
3. Be considerate of others.
4. Keep the environment safe and clean.

To ensure that everyone shares the same clear expectations for behavior, the standards need to be posted in print large enough to be read by fast-moving students. To ensure consistency, the standards need to be reinforced by both the playground monitors and every staff member in the school. If trouble arises on the playground, the standards need to be readily available for review by all parties before corrective action is taken.

Most children and adults will agree that a low level of safety, fairness, and fun on the playground is simply not acceptable. Reminding everyone of these mutual goals can help to keep results at a high level. When the playground works well, it tends to make everyone feel that the whole school is "on track" and accomplishing the mission.

## Troubleshooting for Recess Management Problems

Regardless of how well or how poorly the playground may be functioning, the management of recess time can continuously improve through a process of regular reflection and open discussion. A review of the total picture can reveal needs for additional procedures, communications gaps, or breakdowns in training. The review cycle also needs to include the following:

1. Review of the agreed-upon standards
2. Review of the playground boundaries and the use of various areas
3. Review of key procedures for arrival, equipment sharing, lining up, and departure

## A Specific Plan for Behavior Management

Along with schoolwide agreement on the basic goals, procedures, and standards for behavior, there needs to be a clearly written plan of consequences for violators. The program of consequences needs to be agreed upon by the school staff and communicated in advance to all students, staff, and families. This is often done in newsletters to families and in individual classrooms by the teacher with the monitor present if possible. The following is an example used at one elementary school of a successful behavior management plan that defines escalating levels of consequences.

THE FIVE LEVELS OF CONSEQUENCE MANAGEMENT

1. *Warning:* The student will be informed of the problem and reminded of the consequence for noncompliance.

2. *Time-Out:* The student will be removed from the activity and asked to reflect on what happened. The monitor and the student will discuss the problem.

3. *Consequence:* The monitor will assign an appropriate consequence and contact the teacher and the family.

4. *Conference:* A conference with the student, monitor, teacher, and family will be arranged to inform everyone of the concerns, to hear the student's perspective, and to seek an agreeable solution that will result in the school standards being upheld in the future.

5. *The Principal's Conference:* A conference with the principal, student, monitor, and family member(s) will be arranged. In some cases, the

guidance counselor or school psychologist might be included if those resources are available. This consequence level is reached when the other four levels have failed to be effective and the misbehavior continues. It consists of a comprehensive review of the student's overall behavior and school performance in all areas. It indicates the need for an intervention that goes beyond what the monitors alone can provide. Although it can lead to expulsion from school, it often results in the creation of a mutually agreed-upon contract regarding desired changes in the student's behavior. The contract is reviewed at predetermined points.

## Specific Behavior Management Ideas (for Staff Use Only)

The following list of inappropriate behaviors and consequences is offered as a guideline for monitors. The consequences should be reviewed for consistency with the schoolwide discipline plan and explained to students in advance. The identification of fair and appropriate consequences for misbehavior is an important part of achieving the goal of a safe, fair, and fun recess for all students.

| *Student Misbehavior or Occurrence* | *Appropriate Consequence or Intervention* |
| --- | --- |
| 1. Running in line | Send student to the back of the line with a reminder to follow the rules. |
| 2. Pushing in line | Investigate all sides, separate in line, and remind students to follow the rules. |
| 3. Fighting | Investigate all sides, send to health room with a pass, if necessary. Separate students and have them sit apart to reflect on the problem. |
| 4. Name-calling; verbal harassment | Investigate all sides, separate students, and place them apart to reflect on their misbehavior. Depending on severity, write a note to the front office, summarize both sides, and bring in involved students to tell their version of what happened. |
| 5. Won't line up at the signal | Remind the student to line up immediately, and make a note to watch that student the following day. For a second offense, have the student miss 5 to 10 minutes of recess. |
| 6. Fighting over equipment | Remind the students that the equipment is for everyone to share, and help the students to figure out a way to share the equipment in a fair manner. |
| 7. Playing an inappropriate game | Stop the game immediately, and ask the students to figure out a way to share the equipment in a fair manner. |

| Student Misbehavior or Occurrence | Appropriate Consequence or Intervention |
| --- | --- |
| 8. Injury | Send the student to the health room with a pass or send a note to the office with a student requesting help from a health assistant or an administrator. (Some schools equip the monitor with a portable phone or beeper.) |
| 9. Emergency | Blow the whistle using a predetermined signal for emergencies such as four loud bursts. This emergency signal indicates the end of recess. Students line up and sit on the blacktop to await further directions. |

## General Playground Rules

To help train students to make good decisions and have the confidence to exercise personal responsibility, some general rules are required. The following are some examples:

1. Students may not bring personal toys or other playthings from home for use on the playground.

2. Contact sports such as tackle, touch football, or "keep away" are not permitted.

3. The blacktop area is used for games like hopscotch, tetherball, basketball, and so forth. It is not used for soccer, kickball, or tag.

4. Food and gum are not permitted on the playground.

5. Students must report all injuries to the playground monitor.

6. Students may throw balls and bean bags, but not sticks or stones.

7. Tetherball is not an appropriate game for students in grades one and two.

8. All students must stay on the school property and in the view of a playground monitor at all times.

## Ten Final Tips for Smooth Recess Management

1. Use the school's Behavior Management Plan to set up fair consequences for inappropriate behavior that are consistent with the school's mission and goals.

2. Discuss appropriate activities and games with consistent rules for each grade level with the physical education teacher.

3. Post the Behavior Standards and Playground Rules so that all can see and reference them.

4. Be consistent when addressing behavior and safety issues.

5. Set up a reward system for each grade based on safety and sportsmanship. Safety awards may be based on fewest number of injuries. Sportsmanship awards may be based on fewest number of fights and arguments requiring adult intervention. The reward could be an extra recess.

6. Send families a letter containing the Behavior Standards and Playground Rules. Request that they review them with their children and sign a statement of receipt that is returned to school to verify that this has been done. (Bonus: This document can be helpful in the event that a family conference is required at some time in the future.)

7. Develop a daily and monthly checklist for playground safety that includes an inspection of the grounds for loose or broken equipment, and for trash, glass, pebbles, or stones on the blacktop.

8. Periodically review the Behavior Standards and Playground Rules to make sure they are still appropriate.

9. Ask the physical education teacher to review the recommended games for each grade level as part of the PE class midway through the year.

10. Remember that the two keys to safe playground time are (1) circulate continuously and (2) supervise, supervise, supervise!

# II. Hall Monitoring

There are generally two times during the school day when the halls require monitoring by one or more adults: arrival time and dismissal time. How monitors perceive the purpose of their job not only makes a strong impact on the way they interact with the children but also affects the degree of cooperation and support they receive from the children, parents, and staff. For instance, if monitors see their job as merely crowd control to move kids out of the halls or onto the buses as fast as possible, they might act like traffic robots giving orders. Although this may accomplish the purpose, it is probably a duty most of us would dread!

Now, picture this instead: What if the job of the hall monitor was to make the hallways a continuous reminder to students, parents, and staff of the schoolwide commitment to providing a safe, orderly, and nurturing environment for students and staff? Then the monitor would likely have a more positive focus and might tackle the job with the enthusiasm of one motivated to make a contribution to the school's overall success. Under these conditions, it isn't just "hall duty" anymore! Now it becomes a valuable out-of-class time to informally observe students in their interactions with peers, gather anecdotal data regarding levels of peer-to-peer conflict resolution skills, identify student leaders and isolated students, and observe levels of cooperation and compliance regarding school rules and standards.

## Tips for Successful Hall Monitoring That Contribute to a Safe and Nurturing School Environment

1. Greet students each day as they arrive and say "Goodbye" when they leave.

2. Make an effort to learn students' names and use them.

3. Smile and establish eye contact with as many students as possible. (The hall monitor can do a lot to give students a positive start to their day.)

4. Be attentive to students who seem to be starting the day distressed, and make a note to observe those students the next day in case there is a pattern.

5. Be equipped with a clipboard of morning routines and procedures for such things as using the media center or delivering messages to the office or school nurse.

6. Occasionally, provide recognition of students who demonstrate excellent hall behavior. For example, a few names could be read over the loudspeaker, students could be awarded stickers or bookmarks, and notes could be sent to the student's teacher or family. (Note: recognition for good behavior can be especially valuable during the time new hall standards are being implemented.)

## General Standards and Consequences for Moving Through the Halls

As with recess management, clear standards need to be established for moving through the halls. The following are examples:

1. Always walk.
2. Use indoor voices.
3. Be considerate of others.
4. Help keep the environment safe and clean.

Students also need to be aware of the consequences for noncompliance. Having a clearly defined set of consequences is a great help to the monitor, increases the likelihood of consistent behavior management, and is very helpful for explaining the total behavior plan to parents should the need for a student-parent conference arise in the future. The escalating program of consequences is similar to the playground plan with a few minor twists:

1. An oral warning is given along with a reminder to follow the standards.

2. A hall violation "ticket" is issued to the student. Copies of the tickets, printed on duplicating paper, are provided for the student, teacher, and parent. The hall monitor discusses the infraction with the student and reminds the student of the standards. If a student accumulates three tickets during the school year, a more severe consequence may be needed.

3. A parent-student conference is arranged by the monitor. The conference might also include the teacher, principal, and others as the monitor deems appropriate. The result of the conference might be the creation of a student behavior contract that is mutably agreed upon and reviewed with the student and parent at a later time.

# III. Bus Duty

Getting to the correct bus in a safe and timely manner is a daily worry for many children and parents. Although students who walk home also need safe procedures, the bus students have problems that are unique. An error can cause hours of worry to the child, parent, and school staff.

A smooth schoolwide dismissal time begins in the classroom. Each teacher generally creates procedures that ensure all the students are ready for the buses and, in some cases, even lined up and waiting for a central call. Once called, students need to know they are to walk through the halls quietly in a single line and go directly to the buses.

Some advance planning, after a discussion and careful observation of the current busing situation, can greatly reduce the chances of boarding errors once the students are outside the building.

## Tips for the Smooth Transition of Students to Buses

1. Coordinate a school safety program that consists of older students who are specially trained. Recognize and reward the students for the assistance they provide at the beginning and end of the year.

2. Ensure safe traffic patterns for arriving buses. If possible, assign buses to regular parking spots that students can rely on. Also, provide a recognizable number or animal sticker for the bus doors that will decrease boarding errors.

3. Establish a safe route for family members to pick up their children.

4. Walk the kindergarten and first-grade students to the buses and, as much as possible, remain stationed where they can see you.

5. Develop a nonjudgmental, easy-to-follow plan that is taught to every student regarding what to do if they are having a problem getting home.

6. In addition to having bus monitor(s), the students' sense of safety and positive closure to the school day can be dramatically increased if they know the same adult (for example, the principal or assistant principal) will be outside everyday to see the buses off and wave "Goodbye"!

# Conclusion: Bon Appetit

**N**ow that your head is full of possibilities, it is time to get started. First, look at the concept of improving your cafeteria. Gather a cadre of interested brainstormers and implementers. Begin to sort out which ideas from this book would work for your school. Consider what additional ideas you can cook up with your creative colleagues. As enthusiasm for the project grows, you will find that creating a restaurant atmosphere in your school lunchroom may be one of the most fun and rewarding undertakings you have tackled recently. Once you have had success with transforming your cafeteria, you can use what you learned and suggestions in this book to work on improving other duties.

Not only *can* the transformation of some of the nonacademic business of your school be undertaken, it *should* be. Why? Because you deserve to feel the same comfort and confidence in dealing with children in the cafeteria, on the playground, and in the halls as you do in your own classroom. Both you and the children have a right to relaxing mealtimes and playtimes during the school day. So, begin by believing you can make a difference, start with small steps, and watch what happens. Best of luck, and bon appetit!

# Resource A: Idea Bank

No doubt, you now have many ideas from the previous chapters about how to plan and implement a cafeteria transformation. This section of *You Don't Have to Dread Cafeteria Duty* offers a smorgasbord of additional possibilities. Pick out some activities that sound interesting and discuss them with your implementers to see how you might use or adapt them in your school restaurant.

Following is a list of the activities included in this section:

# Line Walkers

## Description

Playing an exciting game with large groups of children that makes lining up for dismissal from the lunchroom quiet and orderly may sound impossible. Read on! Not only is it possible, it is fun, too.

## Equipment and Materials

- Microphone, preferably handheld

## Procedure

Announce to the children that you are going to teach them a new game called Line Walkers to make waiting in line more fun. As soon as the line begins to form, the game can begin.

- Tell the children that you will be watching for outstanding examples of line waiting (standing quietly and remaining in line). Add that good examples will be called on to "line walk" to any place in the line they choose.
- The selected child can get in front of the line (like a locomotive), at the end (like a caboose), or choose to stand with a friend. It is the Line Walker's decision.
- Other children can also be called on, one at a time, to be Line Walkers, too. Succeeding children may get in front of previous Line Walkers, if they choose.

The game is a lot of fun and very motivating. It can continue for several minutes until the children are dismissed from the restaurant.

## Other Tips

- Once children understand the game and have played it several times, it is advisable to hold off playing until the line gets long and children start to show signs of getting restless.
- The game can also be played on those occasions when children enter the lunchroom early and become bored and noisy waiting.
- If you observe that children are routinely having to wait in long lines to be served, it may be a signal that serving procedures need to be examined to see if changes are needed. The implementation team can meet with cafeteria personnel and an administrator to brainstorm and experiment with ideas that may streamline the procedures.

# Gallery Walk

## Description

Provide something constructive to occupy children while they are waiting in the serving line by posting a rotating display of artwork or other items of interest.

## Equipment and Materials

- Sign with wording such as "East Elementary Art Gallery"
- Cork strips or other means for displaying works
- Rotating works to display

## Procedure

- Hang the cork strip and gallery sign along a wall where the children line up to wait to get their trays and food.
- Invite the art teacher, parent volunteers, class clubs, instructional assistants, or a team of students to act as curators who will select and display artwork.
- Occasionally, children may be asked to vote on their favorites in special displays.

## Other Tips

- Photography exhibits by student photographers could also be displayed in the gallery.
- Poetry may be displayed instead of or along with artwork.
- Special displays could relate to holidays and school events.
- Children may need reminders about not touching the display.

# Clothespin Passes

## Description

Keeping track of students who are out to the lavatory or other places can be a real hassle for the cafeteria monitor. One way to control the number of students who are out at one time is to issue colored clothespins as passes.

Different colors can be assigned for girls and boys for passes to the restroom, nurse's office, principal's office, and other places as needed.

## Equipment and Materials

- Plastic clip-style clothespins (available in most supermarkets and variety stores)
- A basket or container for storage of the clothespins

## Procedure

During a discussion of "cafeteria guidelines," students are informed that they must have the permission of the monitor before they can leave the cafeteria. This discussion should take place early in the year and can be conducted by the classroom teachers.

Students who receive permission to leave the cafeteria are given a colored clothespin pass which is clipped on their clothing and returned to the monitor when their business is completed.

# Cylinder Game

## Description

The Cylinder Game is an activity designed to entertain and provide recognition and reward for tables of youngsters who are practicing the posted standards of good restaurant conduct.

## Equipment and Materials

- 6 to 9 brightly colored tagboard cylinders (The cylinders should be about 12 inches tall and sturdy enough to stand alone in the center of a table. They can be constructed with decreasing diameters so they will nest together for storage.)

## Procedure

Announce that you will teach everyone the Cylinder Game. The paper cylinders should be lined up along the front of the lunchroom in full view to spark interest.

- Explain that you will place a cylinder in the center of some tables where children are doing an outstanding job of following the posted standards for excellent restaurant behavior.
- Let children know that they may keep their cylinder at the table as long as the standards are being followed. Each table may get only one cylinder.
- Notify children that if they temporarily lose their edge of excellence, the cylinder can be snatched away and placed on another table that is demonstrating model restaurant behavior.
- At the end of the lunch period, tables that have retained cylinders are invited to line up first and allowed to leave for recess 3 to 5 minutes early.

The cylinder game is to be played with a sense of fun. The focus should be on the reward aspect. A table that loses a cylinder should be assured that they can gain it back and the host will be looking for an opportunity to return the reward.

## Other Tips

- The lunchroom "host" can add to the fun by wandering around the lunchroom observing and letting children know when they are doing well.

- The host should leave one cylinder out of the game until near the end. This gives all tables hope right up to the end that they may still earn a cylinder.

- A student or special guest may also be selected as the leader of the game who awards cylinders.

- The game should not be played for more than 10 minutes of the lunch period or interest is likely to wane.

## Lucky Lotto

### Description

Give youngsters who demonstrate exemplary restaurant behavior a lotto ticket that entitles them to enter a special drawing for prizes and privileges.

### Equipment and Materials

- Lotto tickets made from tagboard or paper
- Fishbowl or other container to hold tickets
- Table or designated ticket collection area
- Pencils for writing names

### Procedure

- Inform children of the lotto event.
- Remind them of the standards for restaurant behavior and where they are posted for reference.
- Throughout Phase 2 (Maintenance) and Phase 3 (Cleanup and Dismissal), children may be selected to receive lotto tickets.
- Diners who are given tickets go to the collection area, fill out their names on tickets, and deposit the tickets in the container.
- Approximately once every 2 weeks, a public drawing is held to determine three to five winners. Winners can select from several prizes and privileges such as
  — Free dessert, ice cream, or snacks
  — Five-minute early dismissal for recess
  — Other prizes donated by families or community businesses

# VIP Tables

## Description

Use this technique to recognize and reward youngsters who exemplify the positive standards of behavior by inviting them to sit at specially designated tables in the school restaurant for 1 week.

## Equipment and Materials

- Cluster of three to five designated tables
- Tablecloths (for example, red and white checked vinyl)
- Centerpieces
- Place mats

## Procedure

- Designate several tables (as cafeteria space permits) to be decorated and used to recognize youngsters who have demonstrated outstanding restaurant behaviors.
- Invite children to sit at the VIP tables by having their names read out by the principal over the public address system at the beginning of the week.
- Include special decorations and special treats to honor the VIPs.

## Other Tips

- Names of VIPs can be listed in the school menu or newsletter.
- Youngsters who have been invited to sit at the VIP tables can receive VIPgrams that notify their families of the honor.

# Videotaped Stars

## Description

Encourage positive habits in the school restaurant by periodically videotaping model patrons in action. Use the video clips as warm-up activities
at PTA meetings.

## Equipment and Materials

- Videotaping equipment

## Procedure

- Communicate to youngsters that surprise video clips will some-
  times be made during lunch periods.
- Let them know the stars of the shows will be children who are
  practicing the restaurant behavior standards.
- Have a volunteer videotape specific children periodically.
- Use the tapes as opening activities for PTA meetings to show parents the progress being made in the cafeteria transformation.

# Bulletin Board of the Stars

## Description

A great way of recognizing good restaurant behavior on an ongoing basis is to use a large bulletin board outside the cafeteria. The caption can read something like this:

---

★ **Jefferson Cafe's Best**

★ Thank you for:

    Being polite to others ★ ★ ★
    Always walking ★ ★
    Using conversational voices ★ ★ ★ ★
    Leaving the area clean ★

---

## Equipment and Materials

- Designated bulletin board with a colorful background and caption
- Stars for posting
- Polaroid camera and film

## Procedure

- The cafeteria "host" takes pictures of children who are following the standards.
- The pictures are mounted on stars on the bulletin board.
- After a predetermined display time, the stars can be taken down and sent home with the children.
- A note of appreciation for good restaurant behavior can accompany the star and picture.

# Roving Photographer

## Description

Catch children demonstrating good restaurant behavior by snapping quick pictures of good manners in action. Glue the photos on tagboard note cards and send them to parents to express appreciation for individual children's courtesy and consideration.

## Equipment and Materials

- Polaroid or regular camera
- Note cards made from tagboard

## Procedure

- Let youngsters know that photographs will be taken periodically of those who are demonstrating excellent restaurant behaviors.
- Be sure the host is equipped with the camera and a supply of note cards.
- Have the host snap photos during selected lunch periods and jot short appreciation notes on note cards.
- Identify a parent volunteer or older child who will glue the photos onto note cards and be sure they are mailed or sent home.

## Tip

Someone other than the host can be asked to snap pictures and write the notes if being the photographer makes hosting too hectic.

# Stop Signs

## Description

Just as road traffic is managed by signs, movement through school hallways after lunch can be made safer and less stressful by using signs to communicate expectations to large numbers of exuberant children.

## Equipment and Materials

- Stop signs made of sturdy cardboard

## Procedure

The following steps are suggested to encourage orderly movement from the school restaurant to the playground.

- Check out the route that children take from the lunchroom.
- Note places where they need to round corners or head down long stretches of tempting hallways without supervision.
- Place stop signs on the walls at these problematic points.
- Identify a student line leader who will agree to lead the line to the designated stop sign and then STOP until the supervising adult catches up. The leader then proceeds to the next stop sign and waits for the adult to catch up.
- This procedure continues until the group reaches the playground.

# Media Treat

## Description

As an incentive and reward for appropriate restaurant behavior, set aside a special area to accommodate 10 children to eat their lunches and enjoy a viewing opportunity.

## Equipment and Materials

- Cozy designated viewing area
- Two tables or floor pillows to accommodate 6 to 10 children
- Television with VCR
- Video
- Movie passes made from tagboard or paper
- Other prizes donated by families or community businesses

## Procedure

- Advertise a special opportunity to eat lunch and watch a video.
- Select youngsters for the special privilege based on observations of exemplary lunchroom behavior.
- Give the youngsters tickets that entitle them to go to the head of the serving line in order to have time to watch the video in the special area.

## Tip

Either choose a short video or make the tickets good for several days so youngsters may watch the show in segments.

# Dining With Dignitaries

## Description

As a special treat, children who have been identified as exemplary diners can be invited to eat at a table with local dignitaries.

## Equipment and Materials

- Sign or centerpiece identifying a table as the dignitary table
- Name tags for the diners
- Printed invitations

## Procedure

- Identify "dignitaries" within the community who might be willing to have lunch with a small group of children as a community service.
- Schedule one dignitary to come to the cafeteria each week or month for a period of time.
- Let children know that certain diners will be rewarded for good restaurant behavior by being asked to represent their class at a table with a dignitary.
- Devise a method for selecting children for the honor and give the invitations to those who win this recognition.
- On the day of the special lunch, have youngsters who will be at the table wear name tags. It might also be a good idea to have a brief orientation with them to brainstorm topics they might like to discuss with the visitor.

## Other Tips

- The dignitaries do not have to be nationally known stars. Anyone with whom the children might enjoy talking for a few moments would be a good candidate. Some examples are a Little League coach, the local fast food restaurant manager, or a businessperson who makes a product of interest to children such as candy or toys.
- Community people who participate in this project should be noted in the school newsletter or in the local newspaper if a reporter is willing to come to the event.
- If it is difficult to schedule dignitaries from outside the school, youngsters might also enjoy eating with school personnel such as a custodian, physical education teacher, or an administrator.

## Be Our Guests

### Description

Provide five to ten daily or weekly tickets, depending on lunchroom space, to selected children. The youngsters will use these tickets to win invitations to parents, grandparents, neighbors, friends, or other guests they would like to have lunch with them at school.

### Equipment and Materials

- Guest tickets
- Fishbowl or other container
- Preprinted invitations

### Procedure

- Tell children about a new program that involves giving out several tickets that can be used to win invitations to lunch.
- Announce the new event in the school newsletter or at a PTA meeting.
- Interested youngsters may fill out tickets and put them in the container.
- Periodically, tickets will be drawn and those whose tickets are selected will receive preprinted invitations to send to their special guests.
- Guests check in with the host on visiting day and sit with the youngsters who invited them.

### Other Tips

- Invitations can be illustrated and signed by the children.
- Special badges or some other form of recognition can be prepared for the guests.

# Award-Winning Class

## Description

A mascot or special token can be used to recognize classes that have made noticeable improvement in restaurant behaviors.

## Equipment and Materials

- Stuffed animal, banner, bouquet of balloons, or other special symbol of excellence

## Procedure

- Introduce the special symbol of success during a lunch period.
- Tell children a mystery visitor will be stopping by during lunch periods each week to identify a class that is showing growth in restaurant behavior.
- Each week, the principal can conduct a brief awards ceremony over the public address system announcing the winning class for the previous week. The identity of the mystery visitor can also be revealed at this time.
- The class will get to display the symbol of excellence and, perhaps, be treated to some other rewards and honors.

## Tips

- The mystery visitor can be someone from within the school such as the media specialist or a parent volunteer or community celebrity.
- One of the observation tools recommended in Chapter 1 could be used to help in identifying the best class for the week.

## You're a Star

### Description

Recognize good restaurant behavior by providing special appreciation for children "caught" doing a good job of implementing the new guidelines.

### Equipment and Materials

- Cut-out stars
- Table specially decorated with a star theme

### Procedure

- The host distributes cut-out stars to some children each lunch period who are doing a good job of implementing the behavior guidelines.
- Children write their names on the stars and put them in a basket.
- Several children's stars are drawn from the basket each week and invited to sit at the special star table. They may invite one friend to join them.

# Restaurant Helpers

## Description

Consider designating special helpers to spread ownership of the new restaurant atmosphere to youngsters.

## Equipment and Materials

- Slips of paper
- Jar or other container
- Prizes and privilege cards
- Badges to designate helpers

## Procedure

- Explain that children will have an opportunity to become restaurant helpers.
- Invite interested children to put their names on slips of paper and deposit these in a jar.
- Select a few names each week and designate these youngsters as Restaurant Helpers.
- Give children who are selected to be helpers badges and a brief instruction period to explain the kinds of help they can provide in the lunchroom.
- At the end of the week of service, reward the workers with prizes or cards entitling them to special privileges.

# Happy Birthday to You

## Description

Develop a school tradition for recognizing and applauding children's birthdays as part of dining in the school.

## Equipment and Materials

- Posted list of children's birthdays for the month
- Celebration materials such as banners, balloons, birthday napkins, and so forth.

## Procedure

- Invite children to participate in the birthday recognition tradition. Participation in this activity should be optional in respect to any child who does not wish this attention.
- Set aside a particular day each month to celebrate all the birthdays that take place during the month.
- On the scheduled day, have someone put up birthday decorations including the poster with names of birthday celebrants. These can be very simple or more elaborate. A volunteer may wish to be the birthday coordinator to see that this happens on the appointed day each month.
- Decide on special events that will honor the birthday children. These could include a treat such as a birthday cupcake or a small gift like a special pencil.
- Consider including music and see whether the music teacher wishes to be involved.

## Other Tips

Think about giving birthday celebrants the option of sitting at a special table and inviting a family member to join them.

# Interview a Famous Person

## Description

Maintain children's interest and enthusiasm for the new lunchroom by holding special events such as famous-person interviews.

## Equipment and Materials

- Costumed "famous person"
- Interviewer
- Simple stage or soapbox
- Two microphones

## Procedure

- Identify an adult in the school or the community who is knowledgeable about a particular person from the past or present and who is willing to dress up like that person. Some ideas include

    Television personality

    Sports hero or heroine

    Cowboy or cowgirl

    Artist

    Character from literature

    Animal from an endangered species

- On the day of the visit, have the person situated on the stage or soapbox.
- Have someone who has agreed to act as interviewer roam from table to table and take questions from the diners to the special guest.

## Other Tips

- Conduct the interview for only part of the time so that children do not miss their chance to visit with friends.
- Consider including a short skit as part of the visit.

## Featuring Live Entertainment

### Description

Periodically schedule and advertise special entertainment to enhance the new restaurant image and add to the fun and surprises.

### Equipment and Materials

- List of potential guests and entertainers with input from the children
- Whatever accommodations and props the entertainers need

### Procedure

- Advertise the special guest as a Coming Attraction on a child-made marquis outside the school restaurant door. Also build anticipation by promoting the event through notices in the school menu and on morning announcements.
- Schedule the guest to do a 10-minute show on the appointed day. Guests could include

    Clowns

    Costumed characters related to an upcoming holiday

    Child performers such as ballerinas or pianists

    Table-to-table magicians

- Offer a minilesson to help children decide on audience behavior for the particular type of entertainment.

### Other Tips

A local costume shop might be willing to donate the use of one costume per month in exchange for acknowledgments in the school paper and press releases sent to the local newspaper.

# Microphone Manners

---

**The Good News**

Every cafeteria needs one!

There is no better way to communicate with a large group of children.

The microphone
- Provides a quick means for getting youngsters' attention
- Saves throat strain for the host
- Simplifies dismissal time

---

**The Bad News**

Every cafeteria needs one!

They can take away from the relaxed restaurant atmosphere if not used very carefully.

The microphone
- Carries sound into adjacent areas and can disturb classes
- Can instantly destroy positive ambiance if used to express anger or amplify unpleasant tones of voice
- Can encourage group reprimands instead of dealing with just those who need to be redirected

---

## Appropriate Uses of the Microphone

The microphone can enhance the ambiance, not detract from it, if used to

- Greet children as they enter the school restaurant
- Courteously ask children to get dessert, clean up, and line up for dismissal
- Appreciate those tables demonstrating good restaurant behaviors
- Lead children through lunchtime games

- Provide entertainment for 5 or 10 minutes
- Announce special occasions like birthdays
- Recognize prize winners
- Promote upcoming events

## Microphone Manners for Restaurant Hosts

- Begin messages in a way that shows courtesy to the diners. Because the microphone interrupts social conversation, say "Excuse me" or "May I have your attention?"

- Deliver messages in a slow, well-modulated voice. Children should *never* be yelled at or chastised over a microphone.

- Use short sentences followed by brief pauses to gain attention. Long sentences become too hard to attend to in a large, busy setting like a lunchroom.

- Depending on the content of the message, vary voice tone to capture interest. For instance, try high and low pitches, fast and slow paces, or voices that imitate characters. One teacher developed a robot voice that was a no-fail attention-getter.

- Tape-record your lunch "performances" occasionally to monitor how you sound. Be sure your messages come across as positive, clear, and professional.

- Ask a colleague to observe you in action and give you feedback about microphone use.

# Resource B: Reproducible Sheets

# How's It Going?

**Observer** _____    **Date** _____

**Directions:** Circle the number that best describes what you observed in the lunchroom.

1. Children entered the lunchroom . . .

   in a boisterous manner           in a courteous manner

   1        2        3        4        5

2. Routines for getting lunches were . . .

   time-consuming and inefficient      smooth and efficient

   1        2        3        4        5

3. Conversation levels of children were . . .

   loud and unpleasant          pleasant and reasonable

   1        2        3        4        5

4. The table manners of children were . . .

   poor and inappropriate        polite and appropriate

   1        2        3        4        5

5. During cleanup time, children were . . .

   rowdy                           cooperative

   1        2        3        4        5

6. The condition of the lunchroom after children left was . . .

   messy                     clean and neat

   1        2        3        4        5

7. Children left the lunchroom in . . .

   a disorderly manner            an orderly manner

   1        2        3        4        5

**Note:** This survey can be used to assess how well the implementation is going and which specific areas still need improvement. The survey also can be administered periodically and the results communicated to teachers and students to indicate trends.

# Class Survey

**Teacher's name:** _____

**Please engage children in a discussion of the following questions and record their responses.**

1. Name three things your class does **not** like about the cafeteria.

2. List three ways your class agrees the cafeteria could be improved.

3. What else would your class like to say about the cafeteria?

## What Do You Think?

**Directions:** Please write the answers to the following questions.

1. How does the idea of eating lunch in our cafeteria make you feel? Why?

2. How do people treat each other in our cafeteria? What do you think of that?

3. What do you think about how our cafeteria looks? Why?

4. What is the best thing about our cafeteria? Why?

5. What is the worst thing about our cafeteria? Why?

6. What else would you like to say about our cafeteria?

## How Do You Feel?

Directions: Circle the faces that show how you feel.

1. When I walk into the cafeteria, I feel

2. The people that sit with me at lunch make me feel

3. The way the cafeteria looks makes me feel

4. When I leave the cafeteria, I feel

5. What else do you want to say about the cafeteria?

## Step-by-Step Transformation Plan

### Checklist

_____ 1. Meet with administrator for approval and support.

_____ 2. Plan and facilitate an exploration staff meeting to propose the idea, facilitate discussion, and reach consensus on an action plan.

_____ 3. Launch a three-to-five-person Implementation Team to gather necessary observations and provide feedback to the staff.

_____ 4. Conduct a follow-up staff meeting to report the work of the Implementation Team.

_____ 5. Inform the staff about three phases of cafeteria management.

_____ 6. Plan a communication plan to build support from children and adults in the school and community.

_____ 7. Launch the initiative!

_____ 8. Continue meetings of the Implementation Team to discuss the plan's progress and to note problems and accomplishments to communicate to staff.

_____ 9. Facilitate an end-of-the-year celebration to summarize the year's activities and thank all who were involved.

# Action Planning Form

| To Be Done | Individual(s) Responsible | Due Date |
|---|---|---|
|  |  |  |

# Planning for the Three Phases

### Phase 1: Settling

What is working?                     What needs improvement?

_____                     _____

_____                     _____

_____                     _____

### Phase 2: Maintenance

**What is working?**                     **What needs improvement?**

_____                     _____

_____                     _____

_____                     _____

### Phase 3: Cleanup and Dismissal

What is working?                     What needs improvement?

_____                     _____

_____                     _____

_____                     _____

**Minilesson Frame**

**Objective:** Children will demonstrate the ability to

_____

_____

**Modeling:** The following suggestions can help children get a clear picture of the desired behaviors for positive restaurant behavior.

____ Role-play by teacher and child of inappropriate and
      appropriate handling of a challenging situation

____ Skit by children who have had the chance to prepare a
      presentation showing the target appropriate restaurant
      behavior

____ Teacher demonstration with "think alouds" (talking through
      the behavior choices and the reasons for them)

____ Pictures, drawn by students, of the behavior they wish to
      discuss

____ Relevant literature selections to be read and followed by
      discussion of wise and unwise behavior choices

____ Film or video clips that show the expected behaviors in action
      followed by discussion

____ Entertaining demonstrations of restaurant behavior by older
      children or adults (what to do and not to do)

____ Observation of a demonstration followed by brainstorming a
      list of guidelines to use when faced with situations involving
      peer pressure

____ Other _____

**Guided Practice:** Give youngsters a chance to practice target restaurant behavior with your coaching. Choose one of the following:

____ Practice with a partner.

____ Rehearse with a small group.

____ Have volunteers demonstrate in front of the class and receive
      peer response.

____ Provide information about an authentic application of the
      behavior and ask youngsters to explain in their journals
      what they would do.

____ Other _____

**Independent Practice:** Ask youngsters to be aware of the target behaviors in the school restaurant. Tell them you will be asking them to think about their observations and experiences when they return to the classroom.

**Self-Assessment:** Invite children to think back on their lunch experiences and consider how they performed related to the objective. Use one of the following activities after providing 2 to 3 minutes of private "thinking time" for them to reflect.

_____ Complete a journal entry explaining when they used the behavior and how they thought it worked. (Perhaps, pair with a classmate and exchange ideas.)

_____ Facilitate a class discussion of instances involving the behavior and the pluses and minuses of the performance.

_____ Complete a simple self-evaluation form or individual contract such as the one below.

Name _____

Behavior _____

How did I do?

_____ Great

_____ Making progress

_____ Still need to practice

_____ Other

Comments: _____

_____

**Closure:** Congratulate the youngsters on their progress. Comment on additional ways they can practice and develop the skill (for example, at home or in a restaurant). Revisit the skill at other times with additional minilessons and reminders about using the skill in the lunchroom.

# Student-Produced Skit for Informing Classes About New Standards

**Jerry:** Hello. We are from Miss Smith's fourth grade, otherwise known as the Cafeteria Crew.

**Johnny:** We are here to tell you about improving our cafeteria.

**Mickey:** Our goal is to make the cafeteria more like a restaurant. When you are in a restaurant, you must follow the restaurant's standards.

**Jerry:** Standards are like guidelines you must follow to be allowed to eat in the restaurant.

**Don:** Jefferson Elementary now has its own set of restaurant standards.

*Don puts up the chart of standards. Mickey points to the first one.*

**Mickey:** The first standard is to use restaurant voices. That means talk quietly and use indoor voices. After all, you never see anyone yelling in a nice restaurant.

*Jerry points to the second standard.*

**Jerry:** The second standard is to use restaurant manners. That means to treat others with courtesy. And to be friendly. After all, your classmates are your friends.

*Johnny points to the last standard on the chart.*

**Johnny:** The third standard is to wait quietly when going out to recess. When people are leaving a restaurant, they don't push and run. They walk out like they are civilized.

**Mickey:** We need everyone to help by learning these restaurant standards. Tomorrow, we'll be back to tell you about a fun game to help you remember to use the standards. Enjoy your lunch!

Adapted from a skit written by Jerry Long, Dan Everett, and Carey Magee of Howard County, Maryland.

## Cafeteria Rap

This is a rap
and we are stopping by to say
When you come to the East Elementary Cafe
we'll have lots of fun
with great music for everyone
If you follow each rule
you'll be so cool
So don't be a fool
The cafeteria is cool
If you follow each rule

Adapted from an idea by Tommy Wright, Emily Mack, and Jamie Smith of Howard County, Maryland.

# Example of Letter Requesting Business Support

Jefferson Elementary School
Upton Way
Ellicott City, MD 21042
410/936-1111

Scott's Diner
90 Route 1098
Ellicott City, Maryland 21042

Dear Mr. Scott:

We are the fourth grade class at Jefferson Elementary. We are trying to make our cafeteria a better place to eat and visit with friends. One of the things we are trying to do is set up a special table for guests and for kids who deserve a reward. We want to decorate it with place mats and plastic tablecloths and a centerpiece. Would you be able to send us a donation to help buy these supplies? Also, will you please give us some tips for how to make a school cafeteria more like a restaurant?

If you donate anything, your restaurant's name will be mentioned in our school newsletter to our parents. If you can help us, please call the school office. Thank you for your help.

Sincerely,

Cafeteria Cleanup Kids

Adapted from a letter by Mrs. Feustle's class in Ellicott City, Maryland.

Dori E. Novak and Joanne C. Strohmer, *You Don't Have to Dread Cafeteria Duty: A Guide to Surviving Lunchroom, Recess, Bus, and "Other Duties as Assigned."* Copyright © 1998, Corwin Press, Inc.

## CORWIN
## PRESS

**The Corwin Press logo**—a raven striding across an open book—
represents the happy union of courage and learning. We are a
professional-level publisher of books and journals for K-12 educators,
and we are committed to creating and providing resources that embody
these qualities. Corwin's motto is "Success for All Learners."